Decorating Entrances, Stairways and Landings

This edition first published in the UK 1996 by Cassell, Wellington House, 125 Strand, London, WC2R OBB

Copyright © Text Susan Berry 1996

The right of Susan Berry to be identified as the author of the work has been asserted by her in accordance with the Copyright, Designs and Patents Act 1988

Distributed in the United States by Sterling Publishing Co. Inc. 387 Park Avenue South, New York, NY 10016 USA

Distributed in Australia by Capricorn Link (Australia) Pty Ltd, 2/13 Carrington Road Castle Hill NSW 2154

British Library Cataloguing-in-publication Data
A catalogue record for this book is available from the British Library

ISBN 0-304-34611-X   Printed and bound in Spain

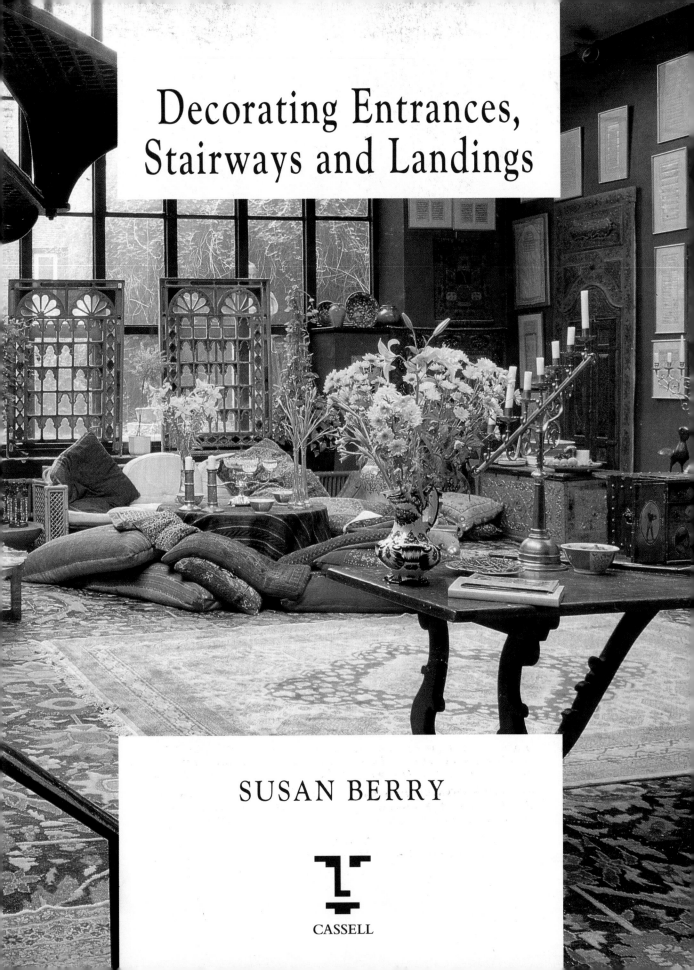

Decorating Entrances, Stairways and Landings

SUSAN BERRY

CASSELL

CONTENTS

Above: This elegant porch, with its black-and-white tiled step, has been painted white, the formality echoed in the tiered topiary pots.

Opposite: This attractive, wide hallway has been given a classical treatment. The diagonally laid black-and-white tiles are an attractive foil for the yellow, black and white paint scheme. The dado area has been papered, and the dado rail and the area above painted.

INTRODUCTION

The entrance and common parts of any house or flat are difficult to decorate, in part at least because such areas are not self-contained. You have to think very carefully, therefore, about the decorative scheme of the rooms opening off any hall or landing and to try to achieve harmony between the respective areas.

People often opt for decorative schemes that are bland and safe, missing out as a result on an opportunity to make something really exciting out of the area. The hallway is, after all, the first impression that any visitor gets of your house and your lifestyle, setting the tone for the remainder of the house.

The first point when considering any decoration scheme for these parts of the house is to decide whether the area is functional. Is the staircase in the right place for a start, and are the doorways opening off the hallway intelligently situated? This has become much more of a problem since houses have been converted into flats, or have been altered to suit different needs, perhaps two rooms being converted into one, to make a large living-room, for example. You sometimes find that the postition of doorways to the new spaces was not properly thought out and that a change will benefit the way that traffic flows.

Front doors, unless you have a porch, can be a source of cold draughts in winter in more northerly climates, and you might be advised to consider adding a porch or altering the position of the doorway to prevent gusts of cold air circulating through the adjoining rooms. At the least, make sure the doors fit well and are well insulated. As a short term measure, one option is to install a heavy-duty door curtain.

The period in which a house or flat has been built is an important consideration when planning a decorative scheme. You do not have to adhere religiously to the ideology underpinning the architecture, but it does pay to be aware of some of its principal period features, so that you do not, unwittingly, mar or counteract its best characteristics. It is even more dangerous, however, to recreate a particular period look in a house that is clearly not of that same era – it tends to look very unnatural and out of keeping.

Opposite: A wide square hallway, such as this one, offers the most scope for decoration, since it gives ample room for furnishings and pictures. A disused doorway has been blocked off, providing a small sitting area.

If in any doubt, keep things as simple as possible and be careful how you use strong or contrasting colours.

Most materials are more attractive in their natural state than when they are tricked out in some way, which is why removing layers of paint or paper to reveal underyling features has become so popular in recent years. Better by far to opt for the natural, unadorned state of the surface in question than to cover it in the wrong fabric or colours.

An important first step is to look carefully at the actual construction and the shape of the fixtures and fittings in your house or flat. Try to work out, in your own mind, whether the lines are attractive or not and in proportion with the rest of the architecture. If they are, find ways to highlight the best points, drawing attention to those features with contrasting paint, perhaps. If you have a particularly fine carved cornice, for example, then pick it out in a colour that contrasts with the walls and ceiling, so that it becomes a major feature. If you have a handsome doorway, with a wide, solid, panelled wooden door, then consider what it has to offer visually when planning the decorative scheme for the hall.

Make sure that these special features are complete and match. It is not much use having a handsome cornice if half of it has been taken down in some previous restructuring, nor is it much use to have one good-quality door in the hall, while the other three or four are of plywood panelling. You need to make sure in any decorating scheme that the basic elements are sound, well-matched and in good condition. However, you could perfectly well have a simple country-style tongue-and-groove board door for the understairs cupboards and panelled doors for the rooms opening off the hallway, but those which serve the same purpose must look unified.

Skirting boards should be of the same height and style, and any door fittings should be of good quality, and they too must match. Although these points sound trivial, it is surprising how often these differences occur and it is just these flaws in detailing which mar any decorative scheme, no matter how well the colours have been mixed and matched.

Much the same criteria apply to the floors in the common parts. Try to keep them consistent throughout the hallway, but you can, of course, opt for stripped wooden boards in the hall and carpet for the stairs and landing. Ideally, try to ensure that the colour chosen for the carpet is repeated in some element of the decora-

Above: A very narrow hallway has been given a uniform treatment in pale cream and white; facilities for storage have been built successfully into a very limited space.

Left: A wide, stone-flagged hallway has been given a 'gardenesque' treatment in soft yellows, blues and greens with a trompe l'oeil effect on the walls, and the windows picked out in contrasting soft blues.

tive scheme for the hall. A stencilled border for the stripped boards in the hall in, say, Indian reds and dark greens could pick up on the russet carpet on the stairs and landing. Another option might be to translate the stencilled border pattern on the hall floor to a stencilled pattern on the stairwell and landing walls. But be careful not to overdo the unification idea – overly matched schemes become too contrived in appearance. One of the short-comings of the current crop of mix-and-match schemes of papers, paints and fabrics put out by many of the international retail outlets is that they are too carefully chosen, leading to a curiously life-less atmosphere when used too slavishly. Decorative schemes should be personal, reflecting individual tastes and choices, and should look as though they have grown over a period of time, being added to and subtly altered over the years, rather than put together during an afternoon in a department store.

Any scheme that has been too carefully co-ordinated fails to look like home, and it is difficult to feel completely relaxed in it. The aim of any decorative schemes is to be visually pleasing, comfortable and restful. The intention, hopefully, is not simply to impress callers with how much you have spent, or how fashionable you are! And if you do not want to spend a fortune again in a short space of time, confine fashionable colourways and ideas to the detail rather than the substance of the scheme, so that you can change it easily when you grow bored with it.

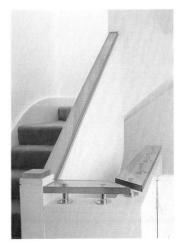

Above: The banisters of the stairway are an important architectural feature of the house, and should be in keeping with the period. Here, in a modern house, the rail is of polished wood and chrome.

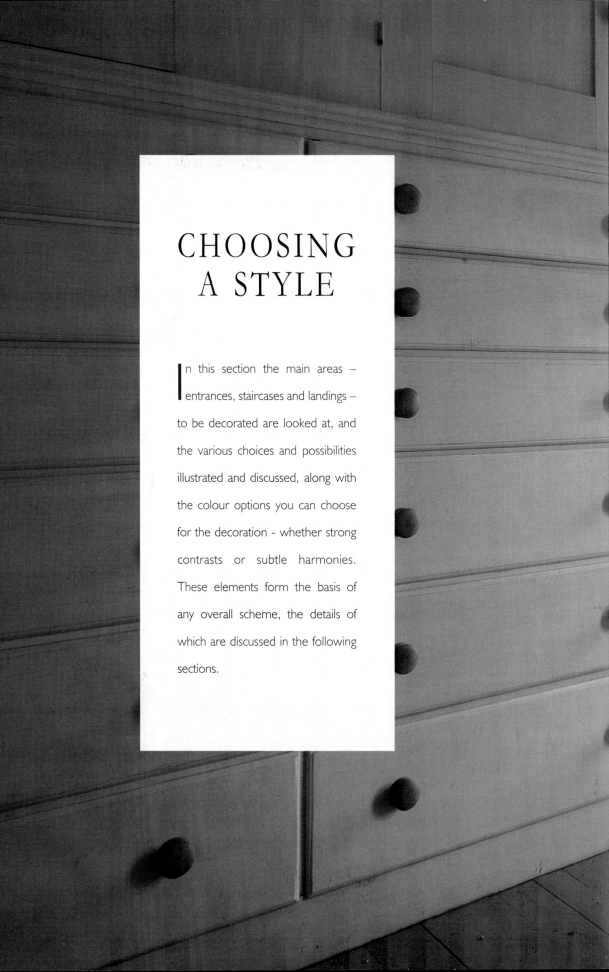

CHOOSING
A STYLE

In this section the main areas —
entrances, staircases and landings —
to be decorated are looked at, and
the various choices and possibilities
illustrated and discussed, along with
the colour options you can choose
for the decoration - whether strong
contrasts or subtle harmonies.
These elements form the basis of
any overall scheme, the details of
which are discussed in the following
sections.

STYLE CONSIDERATIONS

The choice of a suitable style can sometimes seem daunting to the amateur home decorator, given the rich and varied range of possibilities. How on earth, you may ask, do you choose colour schemes and styles? Which is best suited to your particular lifestyle and to the layout of your house or flat?

Firstly, what is the single most important element in the scheme? Do you want something that is practical and cheap, and that will not demand a great deal of time and energy? Or do you want the exact opposite, on which to lavish time-consuming attention and even emotion to create an environment that is extremely personal, reflecting your tastes accurately and satisfying your innermost needs for peace, tranquillity and harmony? Alternatively, do you want to create something striking, different, and visually exciting?

These critical choices must be resolved first, along with your colour preferences, and your tastes for particular materials. One of the easiest ways of reaching a final decision is to run through a quick check - list: which are your favourite colours; what are your favourite materials; do you like your house warm and cosy or cool and light – if the answer is 'yes' to the former, then you could opt for natural woods, warm earthy colours and natural fabrics. If the latter, then you might consider pale smooth walls, bleached or tiled floors, translucent fabrics at the windows and white paintwork.

The climate in which you live should play an important part in your choices, as should the setting – whether town or country, house or flat, basement or high rise. Another important determining factor is the way in which you live – whether, for example, you are a single worker or part of a family. If the latter, any entrance to your house will be used not only by the family, and any pets you might have, but also by the hordes of friends that children inevitably bring into the house, so that wear and tear on any common parts is immense, necessitating some very practical solutions, at least in the short term. Not for you acres of cream carpet and off-white walls: the bicycle-tyre marks, muddy boot and hand prints, and the general fall-out from an average school day, would rapidly turn trying to keep such a scheme in pristine condition into a labour of Hercules.

Opposite: *The soft earthy shades of terracotta complement the rich tones of antique wood perfectly. Colourwashing provides an interesting finish, in which light and shadow help to add depth to the colour.*

Equally, you may not want to create an uninviting, back-to-basics hall simply because the entrance has to cope with these demands. You can find decorative and interesting ways to create a more-or-less vandal-proof environment which also looks good: washable floor tiles in dark but rich colours – burgundy or deep green – with a fairly dark dado area in heavy-duty washable embossed paper, a chair rail in a contrasting colour and perhaps lighter coloured papered or paint-effect walls above. The furniture can be painted and antiqued, which effectively limits the damage caused by any further scuffs or marks; these simply blend into the existing marked paintwork. Darker colour paintwork is definitely a better bet than pale when small children are about. Avoid painting dark colours over white; any marks which are made will show through very quickly, unless you apply several coats of paint.

The English country house style hallway is certainly one to go for, if you want an easy-to-cope-with decoration scheme for family life. Cluttered with boots, mackintoshes, umbrellas and walking sticks, it relies for its attraction on solid old furniture, a simple but appealing decoration scheme and good-quality hard-wearing flooring – stone flags, wood parquet or old, polished boards.

The Swedish country look is also feasible for this kind of family home, but is much lighter and rather more modern in feel. It translates well into many town houses, too, bridging the gap between town and country, with its pale, painted wood, and simplicity of content and form. However, bleached floors, even with washable rug runners, do present quite a lot of work in their upkeep.

A Modernist architectural look, with pure white surfaces, curving modern staircases and an emphasis on form and line rather than on colour is ideal for busy town-dwellers who want to keep the place more or less spotless. But this does not work once it becomes cluttered or obviously lived in and, if it is to be maintained in its pristine state, you will need to ensure there is plenty of storage space.

A more sophisticated town look, with papered walls, attractively carved mouldings, good-quality carpets in neutral colours, is the traditional option for many town flats, but can lack real inventive spark. However, colour choices can play an important role if picked with verve – terracotta and powder blue, perhaps, rather than more traditional colourways.

Above: In a modern house, the stair furniture can become a feature in its own right. Here the curving lines of a chrome banister rail are the perfect choice for this sinuous staircase.

Opposite: The warm tones of the terracotta tiles, the stripped wood cupboards and handsomely carved pillars give this country house hallway a welcoming atmosphere, enhanced by the cheerful yellow of the colourwashed walls.

PATTERN

The other major decision you need to make is the choice between pattern or plain colour. This is one of the most fundamental design points, and you may find yourself feeling equivocal. If you like a little pattern, but not too much, then you might consider using one of the decorative paint effects, such as stamping or stencilling to add a touch of interest to an otherwise plain decoration scheme. If you like lots of pattern, then consider using woven rugs (whether kilims, oriental carpets, Scandinavian or American rag rugs), fabric draped over windows or as door curtains and patterned paper for the walls. You can create some very successful mixes of pattern if you keep the colours to a limited palette – rich ruby reds, forest greens, golds and lapis lazuli blue, for example, or mauves, beiges, taupes and olive greens.

Beware of using very bold patterns in a very restricted space. You are far better off going for a less obvious pattern or a large one in a fairly sober colourway. Remember that dark colours

Right: Plain polished wooden boards, coupled with a neutral colour scheme (the paintwork in yellow ochre and the dado picked out in black and white) give this hallway an air of understated elegance.

recede, but that white in any pattern tends to jump forward at you.

There is nothing to stop you opting for quite bold, strong colours in a hallway. After all, you do not have to live in it, and it might be just the shot in the arm that a dark and dingy space needs. There have been many very successful, Victorian-style schemes, in which a deep red is the principal colour, but avoid teaming it with white paintwork. The contrast is very strong, and if the hallways is broken up with several doorways, you will create a very busy look to it. Better to strip the wood down to its natural state, and use another, lighter colour as a contrast, either for any fabrics, or by dividing the wall into sections, using a different but complementary colour (or a paper with red in the pattern) for one of the sections.

Above: The entrance gives you the first impression of a house or flat. Here, the steps leading up to handsome Queen Anne doorway are flanked with containers on one side and shrubs spreading on to the York stone steps on the other.

17

COLOUR

Deciding on a suitable colour scheme when decorating is often the hardest part, because you are obliged to make a very clear statement about your personal preferences, which can be difficult if you are unsure about them.

Our response to colour is, in part, psychological and different colours affect us in certain ways on a subconscious level. Yellow is generally perceived to be cheerful and optimistic, and a predominantly yellow scheme will lift the spirits. A blue scheme is considered tranquil and restful; green encourages contemplation and is also soothing; brown absorbs energy and can be depressing, as can grey, although both can make quite an attractive display; red is very dominating; orange is restless, and so on. However, in choosing colours, you need to take your own psychology into account. If you are a naturally timid, introverted and quiet person, going for an extrovert colour in your decoration may well embolden and make you more extrovert, although there is danger it could end up dominating you. Exercise caution on these psychological aspects. By far the best solution is to opt for what you know you enjoy and like, rather than what you think is fashionable, since it will probably go out of vogue before you wish to redecorate anyway. Far better, therefore, to opt for a colour you enjoy, that you can live with happily and from which you will derive quiet pleasure.

The other big colour question is: light or dark? You can treat this in two ways: in a dark hallway you can try to introduce light by using pale or pastel colours and by allowing as much light as possible to enter through existing doorways. Or you can make a virtue of a necessity and opt for a dark colour scheme which emphasises the darkness and uses it as an attribute. If you do opt for a dark scheme, at least make sure there is adequate artificial lighting – stairwells must be lit properly for safety reasons.

If you do decide to opt for a strong colour for the hallway area, try to ensure that it links well with the schemes in other rooms. You will not achieve a comfortable living space if you go for a very dominant, strongly coloured hallway and stairwell, if the rooms that lead off are in an array of different colours and styles. You could,

Above: This elegant hallway is an object lesson in stencilling, in both colour and execution. The toning shades of deep green and rust on a paler green ground give an attractive, antique look to the pattern, which makes good use of contrasting stripes and borders.

of course, have each room coloured differently – a yellow hall, a blue living room, a green kitchen, but ideally you would then need to find a link for these ideas to pull them together. You would have to ensure that the styles of all three were compatible, otherwise you might end up with a confusion of colour, pattern and form.

Since the hallway is the place where you greet visitors, it seems sensible to ensure that it reflects your personal style fairly accurately. Leave any frills and fancy bits for guest bedrooms and bathrooms, perhaps, and ensure that the hall is a barometer of your taste and style. If you have a country cottage, and you like outdoor pursuits, your hallway can reflect your lifestyle with pegs for coats, racks for muddy boots, space to store your tennis racquets or croquet mallets, and a colour scheme that works well with these kind of artefacts. Deep forest greens, terracottas and sand colours would look good, as would white with deep coloured paintwork in flat oil paint. Floors could be flagstones, brick or quarry tiles. You could panel the lower part of the wall with simple tongue-and-

Above: Subtle alterations of tone for the horizontal bands of colour on these old plastered walls provide an elegant setting for the antique furniture, and one in keeping with the architectural style.

19

groove panelling in deep colours, which will help counteract the mud-splashes of pets and children.

In a city flat, perhaps with a narrow corridor, a very pale white or cream, with some nicely hung black-and-white etchings or photographs, and a black-and-white tile floor might provide a suitably sophisticated entrance. If you are on the second floor of a block of flats, you do not need to worry about pale colours on the floor getting dirty, as you do in a country cottage where the hallway opens directly to the elements.

CONTRASTS OR HARMONIES

When putting colours together, you have to decide whether they are to harmonize or contrast with each other. Much depends on the size and style of the space. If it is narrow and confined, you are better off opting for colour harmonies, which will tend to enlarge the available space. Colour contrasts divide up space and are useful for reducing the length of a long corridor. You can break up a long flat expanse of plain wall with coloured doors, for example. All sorts of interesting games can be played with colour contrasts: you could paint every door leading off the hallway in a different colour but with coordinating colours for the architraves, for example, or you can reverse the colour detailing.

A very tall stairwell can be reduced in height by dividing it up, using contrasting colours for the areas below the dado, between the dado and the picture rail, and between the picture rail and the ceiling. Similarly, you can add interest to an area and help to enlarge it at the same time by using toning shades of the same colour.

COLOUR COMBINATIONS

As with most elements of decoration, colours and colour combinations go through particular periods of popularity, and certain colours typify distinct periods in history. Robert Adam, for instance, tended to use the bright mid tones of the colours that he liked on his Grand Tour of Italy as a young man, and his colour palette was widely imitated in Georgian England. The Rococo period in the eighteenth century was marked by a colour palette of powder blues, pale pinks and golds, distinguishing it from the sterner, more monochromatic palette of Neoclassicism. The Victorians opted for deep rich reds, greens, golds, as well as tobacco browns, in a masculine, solid and rich palette that reflected their new-found

importance and wealth. The Jazz Age of the twenties and thirties was characterized by smart blacks and whites, the hippie period of the sixties by vibrant oranges and purples, and the 'country look' of the eighties by natural, neutral colours with lots of texture.

What you choose will, in part, be influenced by what is currently on offer in magazines and manufacturers' catalogues, from which you can select elements to combine in your own particular

__Above:__ In this light, airy hallway, a feature has been made of the tiled floor, which incorporates an attractive flower and animal motif, the rest of the decoration scheme harmonizing with it.

way. One of the most successful ways of combining colour is to pick colours with the same tonal values and use them together. Contrasts excite interest, but similar tonal values will help to add unity to a scheme so that it is soothing without being dull. A mid-blue and a mid-green, for example, could be combined in this way, or a soft mid-blue and a deep ochre yellow. Sharper contrasts could be dark blue with a sharp acidic green or bright yellow. Colours that do not officially go together can be used in these contrasts of hue but without the contrast of tone: sands with soft pinks, taupes with mauves, sage greens with rose pinks, perhaps.

Colour and pattern

You can mix pattern and colour very successfully, but you do have to have a very clear idea about what you are doing. If you are less sure, you can still mix them, but it will pay to keep to certain well-defined rules. Try not to mix colour and pattern too freely. If you want to mix pattern, keep the colour palette limited to say two or at the most three colours. You can use the same pattern in reverse colours to good effect, although you must make sure that this does not look too contrived. Another idea would be to use a large pattern and then take an element from it for a smaller pattern, or to reverse the ground pattern.

White in any pattern tends to break up the final effect, which will be dissipated or changed, so you may find it easier to mix patterns that have no white in them. Patterns without white present a far more solid appearance, which is closer to the use of plain colour. The designs of Souleiado – the Provençal prints in rich golds, blues, and browns which never have white combined with them – are one example of this. Here, it is the combination of colours, without white and with which very little white has been mixed, which gives them their density and solidity. You could take one of the colours in the pattern to create a border, or use it to paint a dado area, dado rail, or doors, for example.

Hand colouring of pattern produces some interesting effects, and you can use blocked, stencilled or freehand designs in this way to express your own colour preferences. Acrylic paints, which are available in a wide range of colours, are particularly easy to use and are also very quick drying. See pages 36-40 for further information and inspiration.

Opposite: This NeoClassical hall is decorated in cream self-stripes with a terracotta marbled dado and a Greek pattern acting as a border. Classical plaster busts and a marble hall table complete the effect.

ENTRANCES

The style of the entrance to the house will almost certainly be determined by the period in which it was built and the size of the house. If you are lucky enough to own a double-fronted house, the entrance will almost certainly have gracious proportions, be large enough for you to install furniture in it, and probably have several doors opening from a wide, square hallway. A small terraced house will almost certainly have a narrow, quite long hallway, with the stairs rising either at the end of the passageway or, if the house is very small, the passage may well have been knocked through into the living-room, from which the stairs rise directly. This particular style occurs frequently in artisan's cottages, where space is often at a premium.

How you decorate the entrance, then, depends to a large extent on shape and size, but if there are several doorways opening from it, one of the most important considerations is the creation of a scheme that harmonizes with the view through to the adjoining rooms, and

Right: Softly toning shades of peach and cream have been used for this pretty wooden porch. Its tracery-type woodwork makes an excellent contrast of form with the simple flagstones set in the cobbles leading up to it.

Opposite: This open-plan hallway-cum-living area has been decorated in a simple but elegant style, with the stair treads and woodwork picked out in sage green and the far walls bagged (ragging using plastic bags) in sage green over cream; the dado rail is in white for contrast.

Right: A false arch has been decorated with delicate freehand-painted fritillary and grass images. For the less skilled, the same idea could be copied using stencils or stamps (see page 62-69).

Above: A monochrome scheme in white and black, with a natural brick floor, provides a suitable treatment for this small garden entrance. Simplicity of colour allows the eye to focus on texture - in this case, of wood and brick.

vice versa. One of the simplest and most effective schemes is to pick up particular elements from the different rooms and combine them in the hall decoration. You could, for example, use the different colours of the living room, perhaps painted in terracotta, and the kitchen, perhaps in green, to create a stencilled floor pattern on a stripped wood floor in the hallway. Alternatively, you could create a stencilled border at dado height, or you could use the terracotta and green as the basis for the entire wall colour for the hallway, perhaps with a colourwashed dado area in terracotta and a sponged pale shade of the green over the wall area above.

It is obviously important in any house to make sure that any scheme for the woodwork blends with adjoining rooms, so that the doors, for example, look good when open or shut. One of the simplest solutions is to strip the doors down to the bare wood, if they are of solid, good-quality wood. If they are not, then you can still give them a wood-grain paint finish.

One of the most neglected areas in most houses is the space beneath the staircase, usually given over to a large storage cupboard or sometimes, if it is big enough, turned into profitable use as a shower-room or downstairs cloakroom. It can help, in a small and cramped house, to remove the boarding and open it up for use as recessed telephone area, with a desk and a chair. A surprising feeling of space can be created in this way in a house dominated by long, dark corridors. A lamp on the table, creating a pool of soft light, will also give a warm, attractive glow to the area. You will, however, need to think about finding another space for storage, although you may also be able to fit in a small cupboard.

STAIRCASES

The staircase is usually a much neglected feature in any house. A couple of centuries ago, however, it was all-important. Architects like Robert Adam devoted a great deal of their creative energy to constructing elegant, curving staircases that formed the central axis of the house. Since this feature forms such a major communicating link with the upper floors of the house, it seems a pity not to devote a proper amount of thought, both to its construction and decoration.

If you are converting a house, knocking rooms through into each other, or adding a floor in the form of a loft conversion, you will certainly have to consider the kind of staircase you want and the look which goes best both with the period of the house and your own tastes and needs. One element of the staircase which

Below: Pastel-painted wood in sugar-almond shades provides the theme for this country-style landing; the pale pink runner on the stairs is held in place with brass rods.

Left: A simple, stripped-wood approach allows the vernacular, sculptural construction of this old staircase to be seen to its best advantage.

often goes unconsidered are the banisters and handrail. Some inventive modern solutions have been found by architects to make strong sculptural statements with both the staircase and its safety rails but colour can also play an inspirational role.

Underneath almost every faded and rather worn stair-carpet, there is probably a perfectly sound wooden staircase. It is worth considering how best to renovate this to make a handsome architectural feature. The first task, having got rid of the old carpet, is to remove the layers of old, cracked paint from all the banisters, stairs and skirtings, so that at least you start again from a good, clean surface. You might consider painting the staircase entirely and dispensing with the carpet. Be warned, however, that this can make the house quite noisy and is probably not a good option if you have a large family, with children running up and downstairs most of the day or teenagers returning home late at night! A more modern solution is perhaps to lay sisal carpet, which is hardwearing, and goes well with most decorative schemes, modern and traditional. In traditional halls, it can be used as a base on which to lay

Opposite: Wonderful Gaudiesque curves turn this staircase into a fascinating architectural feature. The two-tone colouring of brown and cream paint, with the rich chestnut colour of the wooden rail and banister is a decorative idea worth imitating for a cottage stairwell.

Right: The simplicity of a handsome wooden staircase needs no further adornment.

Above: Subtle tones of grey-blue paint, polished metal and honey-coloured wood give this minimalist staircase great textural beauty.

Right: In direct contrast to the colour scheme above, canary yellow is used to make a focal point of the wooden spiral staircase.

Opposite: A retractable wooden ladder provides the access to this attic mezzanine floor. Deep blue paint is used as an accent colour for door frames and skirtings, and to back the wooden shelving unit.

kilims or oriental rugs and, being neutral in tone, it will blend well with most colour schemes.

If you are inserting a new staircase, there are many styles and types available to you, although no doubt your choices will be limited by budget as much as any other consideration. If you can afford it, the spiral staircase, with the steps arranged around a single supporting pillar, is particularly space-efficient, but not cheap. These come in a variety of forms, from traditional ironwork to modern, fairly lightweight timber constructions, and some modern metal-mesh forms. If you want a modern look to the house, it is worth investigating the various possibilities. A good metal foundry or an experienced cabinet-maker will be able to design and make one specially for you – at a price. Wooden staircases can also be bought off the peg, and again there are a range of types and constructions, from a straight run of steps to one with a twist. There are rules and regulations governing the tread to riser ratio, as stairs must not be built with such a steep rise that they are dangerous, and you may well have to incorporate at least one or two turns into the staircase to fit it into the available space. Less permanent stairways, in the form of extending ladders, are sometimes used for loft spaces and for galleried bedrooms built into the upper half of a high-ceilinged room. Again, you need to make sure these are safe to use, especially where there are young children in the house.

LANDINGS

Above: Minimalist chic is the key to this landing scheme, where storage, in the form of open hanging space, forms part of the architecture, creating an enclosure for the stairwell.

Opposite: A different version of the same concept provides hanging space on this landing. Note the interesting use of texture in a very monochromatic scheme.

Here again, the space available is often underused and little benefit is gained from it. Much depends, naturally, on the kind of architectural arrangements, but quite often a landing will have a particularly attractive window, whether a large studio type in stained glass, as was common in some of the bigger semi-detached Edwardian houses, or small circular oriel windows, or perhaps a recessed window if the house is a smaller cottage. The windows will give you the opportunity to introduce colour and pattern in the form of curtains and/or blinds. Make sure these fit the window embrasure neatly, thereby enhancing the form.

From the vantage point of the upper storey, the light levels are usually excellent, and the sunlight will often pour in through a landing window to create a particularly attractive effect. Try to take advantage of this by placing a beautiful ornament in the window embrasure or a good piece of furniture beneath it. An arrangement of flowers, for example, looks very striking and will probably be seen better here than in any other room in the house. Being relatively cool, this space also suits flowers better than an overheated living room.

You are obviously limited in any decoration style for the landing by the choice for the hallway, since the areas are linked to each other, but you can also introduce subtle modifications to the landing scheme.

One of the most successful, relatively recent revivals is the tonally matching scheme. You take one basic paint colour – say yellow – and paint the walls in subtle variations of it, so that they blend together. In this way, you could move the decoration scheme on a three-storey house from white at the entrance floor to cream, to ochre, sand and pale terracotta as you move up the floors, linking them all with white paintwork perhaps, and stripped wooden doors. Small repeating items which take one element of the colour, perhaps the terracotta, for a piece of painted furniture in the hall, help to create further links between the schemes.

The photographs, left and opposite, introduce some interesting ideas for creating storage space on landings – a good idea where space is at a premium.

PAINT AND PAPER

The key elements of any decoration are painting and papering. In this section we discuss the basics of both, plus some more elaborate paint effects, using a variety of methods of texturing or patterning the surface of the paint. Some of these are now so well known to need little introduction; others, such as frottaging, for example, are less familiar.

MATERIALS FOR PAINTING

There is now an impressive range of paints available from retail outlets, both specialist and general, and some particularly good colourways. Interest in period architectural detail and the work of various heritage organizations have done much to advance research into the different compositions of paint used over the centuries and the colours popular at different eras.

To the uninitiated, paint is simply a chemical mixture and very few people have much idea about how it is made up. Most know that there are two principal kinds: oil-based paint (which has to be thinned with white spirit or turpentine) and water-based paint (thinned with water); oil-based paint tends to be glossy in finish and is used for woodwork, and water-based paint has a more matt surface and is used for walls.

The introduction of acrylic, water-based paint in forms that are applicable both for matt and glossy finishes, and which can be used for walls or woodwork alike has revolutionized the painter's repertoire. Acrylic has the virtue that it is less messy to use, is more or less odour-free and spills and brushes can be cleaned with water. It does, however, have certain disadvantages. Its rapid drying time makes certain paint effects which involve working into the wet surface tricky to carry out, and the finish it produces is curiously flat; it has very little reflectivity and can give the surface a plastic appearance.

In the opposite direction, at least one paint company is producing paints today that are modelled on the paints of old – using the same ingredients. The resulting paints have a particularly luminous, attractive finish, but they are certainly not the cheapest you can buy. They do, however, come in some truly wonderful colours, most of which seem to blend and harmonize effortlessly.

If you are particularly adventurous, you can mix your own paints, using artists' acrylics for acrylic or water-based emulsion and artists' oils for oil-based paints. This is fun to do and not particularly difficult, but it is difficult to repeat exactly the colours created. The best solution is to practise with a small range of artists' or acrylic colours and use them to tint small pots of white paint until you have mixed a range of colours you like. Take note at the time of the proportions used (very little pure colour is needed to tint a 2.5 litre can) and write it down in a home decorator's notebook, complete with a small sample of the finished colour.

EQUIPMENT AND BRUSHES

It would be meaningless to give a long list of equipment here, since different styles and different jobs require different tools. It does pay, however, to make sure that you buy the best quality paintbrushes you can afford, as fully bristled as possible, since the finished result will be infinitely better. If you bother to buy good brushes, then at least look after them properly, cleaning them thoroughly after use and storing them where air can circulate around

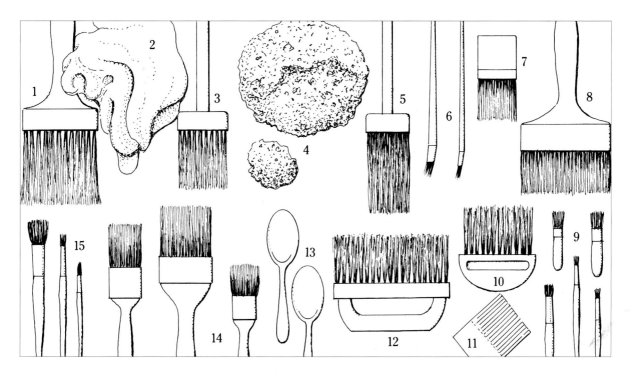

The equipment shown overleaf (with keyline drawing above) shows the full range of brushes and painting equipment.
1 Badger Hair Softener 2 Cotton Stockinette
3 Hog Hair Softener 4 Natural Sponge
5 Indian Hog Hair Flogging Brush 6 Fitches
7 Mottler 8 Gilding / Varnishing Brush
9 Stencilling Brush 10 Dragging Brush
11 Metal Comb 12 Stippling Brush
13 Spoons for Mixing 14 Decorator's Brushes
15 Artist's Brushes

the bristles – hanging on hooks on a shelf in a cupboard, for example, which is also a convenient place in which to dry them.

Most forms of decorating require a variety of brushes. Those shown are ideal for a starter kit, which you can add to as you become more involved in trying to achieve elaborate finishes, some of which, like dragging for example, demand a particular long-bristled brush, known as a 'flogging brush'. A spirit level is more or less essential in many forms of decorating for creating straight vertical or horizontal lines.

Sugar soap, white spirit, cotton rags and a sponge, a roller and tray (if you prefer these to brushes) are all essential ingredients, as is sandpaper and cellulose filler for preparing walls and for woodwork.

A couple of metal paint kettles are also particularly useful in painting. For papering you must have a Stanley knife or scalpel, and a sharp pair of scissors and a plumbline, and a large flat surface to work on.

Right: *Woodwork looks very good when dragged, particularly if the base and top coat are very similar in tone. It gives a lustrous finish to the wood, which is particularly attractive.*

PAINTING WOODWORK

A hallway has a great deal of wood in the form of doors, windows, banisters, stairs and skirtings, so it is extremely important to ensure that your painting techniques are excellent. Attention will be focused on the woodwork and, if it is badly painted, the whole effect will be ruined.

The first step, of course, is to ensure that the wood is in a fit condition to be painted. If the paintwork is cracked, peeling or uneven, you will need to strip it back to the original bare wood. You can do this by using a chemical paint stripper, applied according to the manufacturer's instructions or by burning the paint off with a blow-torch or hot-air gun. The latter method is, without question, the easiest to use on doors and skirtings. You simply direct the blast of hot air on to the paint: this causes it to bubble up and soften, so that it can be removed with a scraper. You must play the gun over the surface, as you would a hair-drier, or you may scorch the wood. Also, if you use a hot-air gun on a window frame, you risk the heat cracking the glass, so it might be wiser to go for a chemical stripper for those areas.

Whichever method you use, stripping paint is undoubtedly time-consuming and laborious. You may, therefore, prefer to hire a professional to do the job for you, leaving you with a clean, ready-to-prime surface on which to work. If you do decide to do the job yourself using a chemical stripper, you must wipe the surface down with white spirit to neutralize any chemicals in the stripping agent once you have removed all the existing paint. Then fill any cracks or holes in the woodwork with wood filler, and sand down to produce a smooth surface on which you can paint. If the existing painted surface is in good condition, rub it down with glass-paper to take off any shine to provide a surface which will take the new paint. Clean it with soap and water, rinse with water, and prepare to paint. Make sure all the surrounds to the door are clean and dust-free, otherwise your paint-brush will pick up all the dust when loaded with wet paint. Make sure that you paint windows first thing in the morning to allow time for the paint to dry so that they can be closed at night. Use a small wedge to hold doors in an open position so they do not move when you work on them.

It is important, if you are using gloss paint for woodwork, to pay great attention to preventing runs and drips occurring, when painting panelled doors, or window frames so be especially careful not to overload the brush. There is a correct way to apply gloss paint: first paint down with the grain, then across and then back down again. This will give a smooth, flat finish. When painting windows, it is important to leave a very fine overlap of paint on the glass to protect the woodwork. This is extremely difficult to do accurately, and the easiest way to ensure a straight edge is to use masking tape for the job, which must be removed before the paint dries. Then pull it off in one quick movement, like removing an elastoplast, to avoid smudging the paint or getting the paint covered tape on any other surface. Have a bin handy for the used tape.

PAINTING ORDER FOR FLUSH DOORS

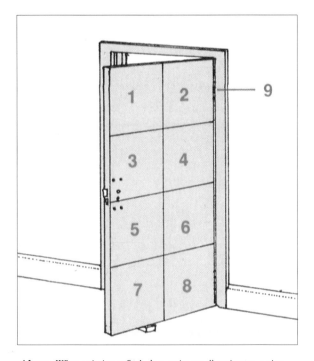

Above: When painting a flush door, paint small sections at a time following the order shown here as this will minimise the risk of the paint running.

PAINTING ORDER FOR SASH WINDOWS

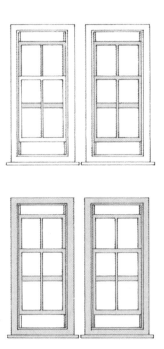

Above: Sash windows are always awkward to paint so follow this sequence. Lower the top half of the window almost to the sill and push the bottom half up over it. Paint the top sash and then push it back up to complete it. Next paint the lower sash before finally painting the frame and runners.

PAINTING ORDER FOR PANELLED DOORS

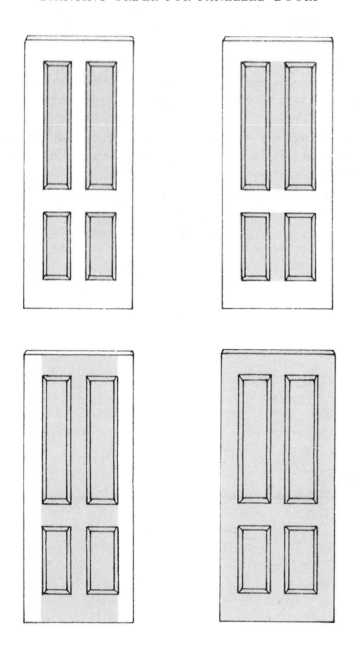

Above: *This sequence shows the order for painting a panelled door. By following it you will always be working towards wet edges enabling you to join them smoothly before they dry.*

PAINT COLOURS AND MIXES

Two of the hardest tasks facing any amateur decorator are picking the right colour for the situation and mixing together colours that work well in combination. One problem is that we all have received ideas on what colours 'go' together and are frightened to experiment as a result.

Colours do not perform in large quantities in the same ways they do in small ones; picking out paint colours, for example, from a paint chart is all very well, but the little rectangles of colour are all the same size. If you choose, for example, to paint the dado area in one colour (which is about one third of the wall) and the rest of the wall in another colour, you are not contrasting similar areas of colour. To your surprise, and possibly horror, the effect when you get the paint on the wall is not at all the same as you envisaged it from the colour chart (not helped either by the fact that the paint in the tin is not exactly the same as the colour chart!).

The reason for this is that colours perform differently when seen against each other and will also perform differently depending on the area they are covering. The only way to achieve in microcosm the effect you will achieve on the walls is to use a box of paints or some crayons, and colour in the areas in a notebook in the proportions you intend to use them on the walls. Alternatively, you can now buy little sample pots of the paint you intend to use and you can create a sample board using these colours.

It does help if you understand something of the composition of colour and of tone and saturation. These terms all sound rather technical, but we are really talking about the intensity of colour and its lightness or darkness. The intensity is derived from the pigment that creates the colour, while lightness or darkness are achieved by the addition of black or white to it.

The pure colours are red, blue and yellow: the primary colours. All other colours are a mixture of these in various forms, with or without the addition of white or black. If you are mixing colours, you will find that the ones that have the greatest intensity and the ones that have white added to them tend to advance and those that are darker tend to recede. It pays therefore to use very bright colours in smaller quantities than darker, dingier ones, otherwise you will find they dominate the colour scheme. The colour palette, below, shows some of the ways in which you can manipulate intensity and tone to produce different effects.

If you are putting colours together for paint effects in which one colour is painted over another colour rather than alongside it, you need to consider the effect that the combination of colours will have on each colour. A blue over a yellow will produce a

These colour wheels will help you to understand the basic principles of colour.

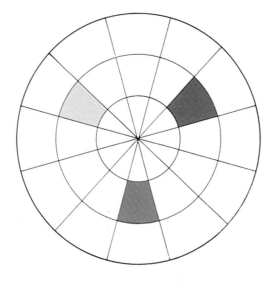

Primary Colours: *Red, yellow and blue are the basic colours that cannot be created from a mix of other colours. However, every other colour can be obtained by mixing them together in varying proportions.*

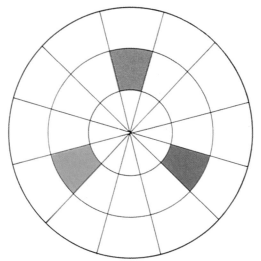

Secondary colours: *Orange, green and violet are created by mixing two primary colours in equal proportions. Therefore red and yellow make orange; yellow and blue make green and blue and red make violet.*

greenish appearance, a red over a green will have a brownish effect and so on, reflecting the ways that colours mix naturally. You can use these effects to create interesting colourways with paint effects. For example, if you want a greenish look without going for green itself, consider frottaging an ochre over a dull blue base coat. You will have to experiment with boards, because it is impossible to be precise about the effect until you have tried it out first.

If you want to play safe with colours in paint effects, use white as the base coat and put a coloured glaze over it. There is another advantage to this technique. You can simply change the colour of white walls by painting a glaze over the base, then working into it with a sponge, brush or cloth (see page 48-52). If you are going to apply this principle to a coloured wall you no longer like, it is a good idea to practise first, in case the base colour, showing through the top glaze, produces a colour effect that you had not anticipated.

Opposite: You can, without too much difficulty, mix your own paint colours; if you are copying an existing colour, it is sometimes unavoidable. Acrylics can be added to water-based paints, artist's oils to oil-based ones. A very small quantity of some colours (particularly Indian red) goes a long way, so experiment drop by drop if adding them to a white base coat.

Right: If you want colours that harmonize then choose the hues next to each other. For a really bold apprach choose the opposite, contrasting hues. For rooms with cold north-facing light, pick a colour scheme from the warm section of the spectrum.

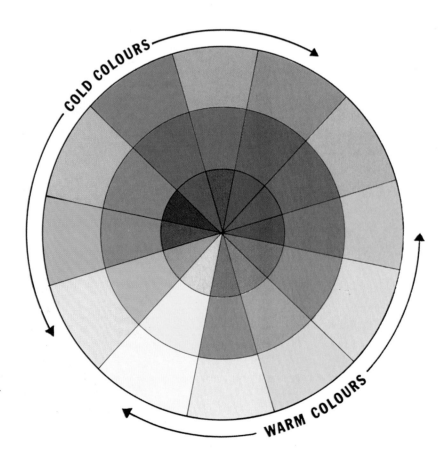

PAINT EFFECTS

Apart from the traditional and straightforward application of a uniform painted surface, using an appropriate paint finish, you can opt for any one of a whole range of paint effects. These have become extremely popular over the past few years, and some of the techniques, in particular ragging, sponging and dragging are now in common currency, rescued in the last decade from many years of neglect.

At one time, any properly trained house painter was versed in these techniques and knew also a great deal about the composition of paint. These days, with new forms of paint being introduced more and more frequently as the chemical industry finds new solutions to former problems – the length of time paint takes to dry, for example – you need to take care that the paint you use for the techniques is appropriate for the purpose.

It helps before embarking on any of these techniques to understand the basic elements on which they are founded, and why they were developed.

The main aim of a paint effect is to change the surface of the paint so that either the texture is varied or the light catches it in a different way. An all-over painted surface is flat, and uniform. This can have virtues in itself – it provides a simple, clean background, rather like a painter's canvas, enabling you to play with the other decorative elements at will. This could be extremely helpful in a room with plenty of furnishing interest. In a hallway, where there is less space for such additions, you may well decide that paint effects could be the answer to creating interest on the only major surface at your disposal – the walls.

There is a range of paint effects that are quite similar in execution, it is simply the object you use to make the mark that differs. These are sponging, ragging (and its variations, muttonclothing and bagging) and dragging. All of these are, or can be, executed, in the same way. You first paint a base coat on the surface (in either an eggshell finish or silk emulsion) and, when this is dry, you start to paint (in smallish square areas) a glaze coat, which is thinner in composition than the base coat. You then use a brush (with long

Opposite: This elegant hallway has a marbled panel inset into the end wall. Marbling is one of the most decorative paint effects, but to do it well requires considerable skill as well as close observation of the graining pattern of real marble. Simpler paint effect techniques are given on the following pages.

soft bristles for dragging, a sponge (for sponging) or a cloth (for ragging) to remove some of this second coat of wet paint, so that the base surface shows through.

It is not, in fact, difficult to do but it is hard to get it to look particularly smooth and even throughout. There are various tips and tricks you can use to secure a better result.

The first is to make sure the second glaze coat is applied in smallish areas, so that the paint stays wet throughout. If you are using an acrylic glaze over a vinyl silk base coat, for example, it will dry relatively quickly. There is no way you would be able to apply the coat of glaze to the whole wall and work into it with your brush, sponge or rag. By the time you got half way across, some of it would be dry.

Oil-based paint and glaze dries far less rapidly, which is why it is often chosen by professional decorators. It also produces an attractively sheeny finish, but this very sheen, unfortunately, also shows up imperfections, so for the amateur or first-time painter it may be better to opt for a water-based base coat and glaze, working in small areas to make sure that it does not dry before you finish the job. If

PAINT EFFECTS
Below are some of the principal types of paint effect – the different ways of breaking up the surface of the paint.

Sponging off: *a white base coat has been sponged in Indian red, partially removing the wet glaze with a dampened sponge.*

Ragging off: *a white base coat has been glazed first with sage green and then with a bluish green, both ragged off with a dry rag.*

you like the sheeny finish, you can always varnish the finished effect with a water-based acrylic varnish, which is completely colourless.

Many of the paint effects can be varnished afterwards to make them more durable. Since they take quite a long time to create this is a sensible precaution. The surface can then be wiped and will last as long as you want. Repainting, which you have to do every few years with emulsion paint, can then be safely delayed until you grow tired of the colour scheme.

Another advantage of using paint effects is that, because the surface does not have a uniform finish, normal wear and tear does not show as much and can be easily patched over. This has considerable advantages in a household with young children, or in a townhouse with no backdoor, where all large and unwieldy objects come through the hall, with resulting damage to the walls.

An ever-increasing range of paint types is being produced, some of them developed specially for different kinds of paint effect, to make them easier to work with and quicker-drying. It is always worth experimenting with new products, but do try them out on a sample board first.

Stippling and ragging: *this effect is a combination of stippling, where a coarse bristled brush is dabbed on the wet glaze, marking it lightly, and ragging, which blurs the effect slightly.*

Cheeseclothing: *very similar to ragging in execution, this technique simply uses a fine-woven muslin or cheesecloth to remove the glaze, leaving a finer, more diffused looking mark.*

How to Sponge, Rag and Mutton-Cloth

These techniques are broadly similar; they simply produce a slightly different finished look in each case. Sponging, shown on page 50, produces a soft, blurred mark; ragging has a more obvious larger mark, with the odd line in it, while bagging creates a more sharply defined outline and mutton-cloth a much softer, finer effect.

One of the other problems with all of these techniques is that it is easy to get a build-up of paint on the very material you are using to remove it. It is imperative that you throw away the item as soon as it starts to become clogged with paint, or you will find that the mark you are making changes in character.

A certain amount of panache is required to make such effects successful. It is important to try first on a small area of wall, or buy some hardboard, then practise until you are satisfied with the marks you are making.

The areas that are most difficult to deal with are the corners of walls and the areas near skirtings and ceilings. You will need to use a piece of cardboard in one hand as a mask so that you do not mark the adjoining paintwork. If you cannot get the object (sponge or whatever) into the corners, simply go as close as you can and then touch up these areas with a paintbrush afterwards.

It does not take a great deal of imagination to work out that you could experiment with the object you are using to create different effects of a similar nature. Discarded lace articles, for example, might create an interesting effect, as might an old string vest.

Frottage, shown on pages 53-55, is a variation on the same theme, only more of the paint is removed than in the effects shown here. Colourwashing and dragging are dealt with separately (pages 56-9 and 102-3) because they require a different kind of treatment. In the case of colourwashing, you are simply using thin coats of paint brushed over each other. In dragging you do not remove the paint but work into the surface to create a particular effect.

The success or failure of these techniques entirely depends on the composition of the paint – it must be of the right consistency to allow you to move it around easily with either paper, brush or rag, and have sufficient drying time which will allow you to work into it as necessary.

FROTTAGE

One of the best effects for hall walls is frottage, which is a rough and ready look that resembles the way that plaster sometimes appears when you have stripped off layers of paint. It is roughly mottled and creased, and is most successful when you pick two colours for it that are fairly close and harmonize well – blue and grey, perhaps, or sage green and yellow ochre.

It is done by applying sheets of newspaper to the wall while the paint is still wet, so that most of it comes off w hen you peel the paper off the wall shortly after you apply it. It is extremely quick to carry out, easy enough for a beginner to do, and provided you are fairly consistent about how long you leave the paper applied to the wet paint each time you move along the wall, the effect works extremely well.

You can vary the effect by varying the length of time you apply the paper. The longer you leave it on the wall, the more paint adheres to it, and when you remove it, so less of the second coat of paint remains on the wall.

HOW TO FROTTAGE A WALL

This technique is easy to carry out. It consists of removing a layer of wet paint with newspaper, but it is messy (you need to be armed with several large bin liners for the discarded sheets of paint-coated paper) and you also need to work quickly. It will help if you can do it with a partner, one of you painting, and the other removing paint with the paper. You should work in areas just slightly larger than the sheets of paper you are using.

Use vinyl matt or silk finish for the base coat with a traditional water-based paint over it, which is then frottaged. The finished effect, when dry, can be covered with a coat of acrylic varnish.

Dilute the paint so that is fairly runny (about 4 parts of paint to 1 of water) and do a test run on a piece of board to check its consistency, and to see how much comes off with the paper. The length of time you leave the paper on the wet paint before you remove it will determine how marked the effect is. The longer you leave it, the more contrasted the effect.

FROTTAGING

With its rough and ready effect, frottage makes a good finish for a dado area, and also provides a good base for an unstructured stencilled effect, using overlapping stencils.

1 Apply a coat of paint over the base coat in a roughly criss-cross manner. For a smoother effect, apply the paint more evenly.

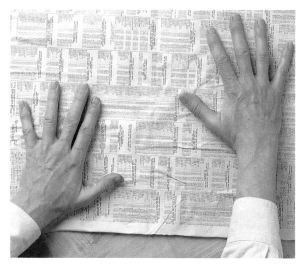

2 Place the sheet of paper on the surface and smooth across it with the flat of your hands. Do not rub it or press your fingers into it, or else you will get oddly circular marks.

3 Keep the paper in place for about 30 seconds (the time will vary depending on the effect you want to achieve) and then remove it and throw it away.

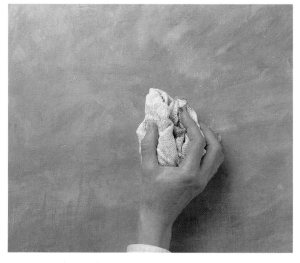

4 If you want a smoother effect, remove some of the paint with a damp cloth. Alternatively, complete the wall, allow it to dry, and then paint over the area with a paler-toned water glaze to knock back the colour contrast.

FROTTAGE COLOURWAYS

These frottaging effects have been created using different combinations of colours. Some have been achieved with just two coats of paint and some with three.

This effect has been created over a burgundy base coat with first an ochre coat frottaged over it and then an Indian red one.

This effect has been created using a royal blue base coat, with a mid-green coat frottaged over it.

This has been done with a mid blue base coat and a coat of stone frottaged over it.

This one has an Indian red base coat, with shades of ochre and then grey applied over the top.

COLOURWASHING

This is another reiatively quick and easy paint effect and you do not need to particularly purist about it. It relies for its appeal on a couple of coats of very thin paint, loosely applied, and its chief charm is the resulting variation in colour and brush effect, which makes the surface a great deal less matt and bland than is the case with traditional painting.

Watered-down emulsion paint is the medium and, as a result, you will need to cover the floor area and any furniture or fittings, because splashes are inevitable. The best colourwash effects are obtained by using two or three colours that are fairly close in tone and saturation – perhaps blue greens and greeny blues painted over each other, on a white base coat, or terracotta and rust on an ochre base. You will need to experiment with the colour combinations to get the effect you require, because it is not a precise formula, and a lot depends on paint thickness and how you work.

To make colourwashing serviceable for a hallway, you should varnish it afterwards, once it is completely dry, to protect it and to provide a surface which can be easily wiped.

The colourwashed effects shown opposite were created using traditional water-based paints and acrylic glazes. The aim of a colourwashed effect is to build up layers of translucent colour in a roughly brushed finish. Unlike painting with flat emulsion, when the aim is to get the most even finish possible, colourwashing emphasises variations of depth of colour. The skill, however, comes in brushing out the glaze after you have applied it, so the finished effect is smooth-looking.

To get the most translucent effect, the glaze should be thin and runny. The thinner it is, the more translucent the effect. Unfortunately, the more messy and difficult it will be to work with, so it is best to arrive at some kind of compromise. Traditional decorating books instruct you to mix the glaze with one part of paint to eight parts of water. For an amateur, one part of paint to four parts of acrylic glaze (itself mixed with water, according to the instructions) is always a good recipe. Do a test on a piece of primed hardboard to check the effect first.

Opposite: If you have a large enough hall you can create a small, extra living area. The orange colourwashed walls set off the elegant dresser beautifully.

You can build up several layers of colour to achieve some of the effects shown opposite.

When you are working, cover areas about 2ft square (60cm by 60cm), leaving a wet edge (a margin of unworked paint) around the areas you are working into which you can then feather the paint in the next square, so that you do not get tide marks. If you do inadvertently create a tide mark, rub over it straightaway with a damp cloth.

COLOURWASHING

Build up the surface using repeated layers of thin paint, brushing out any unevenness.

1 *Over a vinyl silk base that is completely dry, roughly brush out a glaze (made up of 4-6 parts of glaze and one part of coloured water-based paint).*

2 *With a dry brush, while the glaze is still wet, smooth it out in broad light sweeping strokes. If necessary, allow the glaze to dry a little further and, with a dry mutton cloth, work in a criss-cross fashion, removing further glaze. Varnish with acrylic varnish.*

3 *Add a further glaze coat in a toning colour, brushing it on roughly as in step 1.*

4 *Brush the glaze out as in step 2, and give a final coat of acrylic varnish. If you wish to apply a third coat of colour for a really rich effect, repeat steps 1 and 2 again with a third colour.*

COLOURWASH COLOURWAYS

These examples of different effects and colours created with colourwashing show just a few of the variations you can create. Colourwashing is an ideal base for a range of different effects, including stamping (see page 66-69) and stencilling. You can also colourwash floors (see page 56-59) as well as walls, on which you can create similar effects, using water-based wood stains.

This colourwash has been carried out over white silk emulsion basecoat with one coat of Indian red glaze.

This colourwash effect has been carried out over an off white silk emulsion base coat, with a single coat of glaze in yellow ochre.

This colourwash effect uses a pinky-beige base coat, with a colourwash of grey-blue over it

This colourwash effect has been achieved with two coats of glaze over a greenish-grey base coat, with a first coat of Indian red glaze and a second coat of grey glaze.

STENCILLING

Another form of decorating walls is to create surface pattern rather than the more textural effects discussed earlier. You can do this in several ways: by buying paper, which already possesses a ready-made pattern, or by making the marks yourself with paint. Of course, there is nothing to stop you taking a leaf out of any three-year-old's vocabulary and making the marks yourself with a pencil or crayon, and making a series of naive drawings. Atlernatively, you can, if you have the talent, paint elaborate murals, which if done supremely well, could turn your hallway into a copy of the Sistine Chapel! This is not, however, an advisable method unless you are very sure of your talent; nothing looks worse than badly executed freehand painting.

It is quite easy, however, to get attractive and satisfyingly original results using pre-cut stencils or rubber stamps which do not demand such a high level of skill. But some kind of artistic eye is required, since nothing looks worse than ill-chosen stencils or stamps in garish colours.

For stamping or stencilling, it is probably best to take a reasonably minimalist stance. Do not cover everything in sight with stencilled patterns, do not go for massive draped swags and borders, and keep the colours muted and fairly simple, at least until you are sure you know what you are doing. If you keep things simple, you can opt for more strident contrasts of colour, but in the first instance, subtlety is more likely to pay off than outright bravura effects.

You can buy stencil cards with ready cut-out patterns (but take care as some are frankly hideous) and you can also buy ready-made stamps. If you have the energy and inclination, you can even cut your own stamps and stencils to achieve a truly individual effect. Deciding where to use the stencils is as important as the chosen pattern. They can form borders – for example at skirting, chair rail, picture rail or cornice height – or they can create panelled areas on the walls, or frame a door, for example. In more elaborate forms, they can be used to create the equivalent of wallpaper, perhaps in striped rows. In a hallway, be aware that you probably have a large expanse of wall to cover and tailor your ideas to suit the time you have available.

Opposite: The architrave of this archway has been decorated in a freehand, Rococo design, but it would be easy to copy using a basket, flower and rope style stencil. The soft subdued colours are all part of the charm.

MAKING YOUR OWN STENCILS

Stencils are not difficult to make; the hard part is to choose a decorative motif which will actually make a successful stencil. You can only do this after you have tried to stencil, because the drawback of stencilling is the tendency of paint to creep under the stencil card, blurring and spoiling the finished image.

This means that any design has to have quite large white spaces (these are the bridges of the card), so pick designs which will translate well when cut or drawn in this manner. There are various books of stencil patterns that have been around since stencilling first came into fashion in the eighteenth century (many such books are published by Dover). Even if you do not want to copy the stencils, a good look at these examples will help you understand what works as a stencil pattern and what does not. It helps, too, if you can decide which kind of image you want. Do you, for instance, want something that reflects nature – fruit, flowers, birds and beasts, perhaps – or simple geometric patterns, such as those found on Moorish tiles or on an Indian blanket? Geometric patterns are obviously easy to devise and to cut; they can look effective if painted in an attractively graded colour palette – soft Indian reds, dusty blues and sage greens. Japanese pattern books also

CREATING A STENCIL
You will need some oiled card or acetate (oiled card is easier to work with, but you can see through acetate so you know exactly where the stencil is being positioned when you fix it to the surface) and a scalpel or Stanley knife to cut the stencil out.

1 Choose a simple design with no particularly narrow elements and, using tracing paper, draw the outline of the image by laying the tracing paper over it.

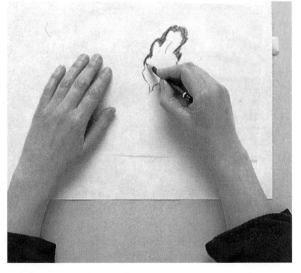

2 Go over the traced design with a very soft pencil, such as a 2B, to bring the image out on the reversed side to make a transfer.

provide useful examples, because the broad brush strokes of the painting lend themselves to this kind of stencil making.

The paint you use for stencilling is important for the final effect. Some experts use car-spray paints and spray through the stencil card. This is effective, because the spray is diffused and soft, but it is not easy to do. Runs, dribbles and splodges occur and car paint is toxic and smelly to use. Better, by and large, to go for simple water-based paint. You can buy stencil paints, which are extremely expensive, or you can make your own up, adding a bit of PVA to some emulsion, to make a slightly stickier paint. You do not have to buy the paint colour, you can create your own without too much trouble by adding acrylics to plain white water-based paint (see Mixing paint, page 44-7).

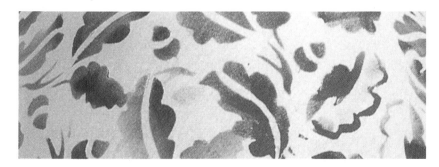

The finished oak leaf stencil painted in raw sienna on a cream ground. As you can see, the varying density of the stencilled image is part of the charm.

3 Turn the stencil back to the right side, fix it on the oiled card with masking tape, and then press through the outline of the design with a biro, so that it transfers on to the card.

4 Cut the stencil out of the card with a very sharp scalpel blade or craft knife. Make sure you have left a good-sized border round the stencil to make it easy to work with.

63

CREATING LEAF PATTERNS

You can make interesting effects, using a form of reversed stencilling, by applying leaves to the wall, painting over them, and then removing them, so that the leaf shapes are revealed in a different colour. There are various ways of achieving this effect, but if you are painting a large area, it is simplest to go for a very random effect.

1 Collect a large pile of variously shaped leaves before you start. Paint the base coat of the area and allow it to dry. Then, using a brush or a narrow roller if you prefer, and the second colour of paint, to a fairly thin consistency, hold the leaf on the wall with one hand and paint over it with the roller and brush. Remove the leaf once the area has been covered and hold it at an angle against the wall fairly close by. Work over the area until you have created a reverse leaf pattern throughout. You can leave the effect at this stage if you like.

2 To create a more blurred effect, allow the first coat to dry and then repeat with more leaves and a very thin colourwash of paint in a toning colour, allowing some leaves to overlap the first pattern. When it is dry, varnish as necessary.

3 To create a more blurred effect, allow the first coat to dry, and then repeat with more leaves, and a very thin colourwash of paint in a toning colour, allowing some leaves to overlap the first pattern. When it is dry, varnish as necessary.

Here a fern frond has been used to create a reverse stencil by tacking the actual leaf to the surface before sponging over it. The leaf image remains sharp and distinct.

In this instance, several different leaf forms have been used, tacked to the surface with successive layers of colour-washing, so that the images become blurred and diffused.

STAMPING

Using a stamp of some description to apply paint to a painted surface to create surface pattern is a technique almost as old as time. It is, in many ways, closely allied to printing techniques, where the painting medium, or ink, is applied to a block and then pressed on to the appropriate surface, be it paper or fabric, to create the image.

To make the stamp, you can use simple household objects, such as a piece of old sponge, or you can carve out simple designs with a sharp knife in the cut surface of a root vegetable, such as a carrot or potato. You can also use objects, such as a cork, to create the design.

It is difficult to create a completely uniform print, no matter what type of block you choose, and half the attraction of stamping is the varied effect that you create owing to the slight unevenness of the stamped image.

It often helps to give the stamped effect a wash of watered-down

BLOCK STAMPING:

Printed block patterns work well as a dado decoration and are quick and easy in a rough and ready chequerboard pattern to apply using a cellulose sponge as the tool for the decoration.

1 Pour the paint to be used for the coloured blocks in a roller tray and then dip one surface of the sponge square into the paint, wiping any excess off on the edge of the roller tray. Create the pattern by dabbing the painted surface of the sponge lightly on to the base board, creating a chequerboard pattern, with the edges of the blocks just touching.

white paint afterwards, which helps to iron out the grosser differences in the amount of paint applied to each image, and also creates an attractively aged appearance to the pattern, rather like an old fresco.

Stamping is particularly useful since it can be used on whatever surface you choose, whether walls, floors, fabric or furniture. If you wish, you can buy quite elaborate rubber stamps (for addresses see page 143), and stationery firms will also get your own designs cut to order, if you wish.

MATERIALS FOR STAMPING

You will need a reasonably thick type of paint for stamping - one of the new traditional-style paints is ideal, as is stencil paint. You will also need a small roller to apply the paint to the stamp, and a tray or sheet of glass to use as a base to apply the paint to the roller.

BLOCK STAMPING A WALL

You can make a very successful design for, say, the dado area of a wall with a simple block cut from an old cellulose sponge. The one used for this simple pattern (and those shown on pages 68) was a 3in (8cm) roughly cut square. Once you have painted the base coat

2 *Clean the sponge thoroughly while the previous coat is drying, and then repeat the process with a second, toning colour. Overprint some of the block, but not all, leaving spaces here and there for a third colour.*

3 *Allow the previous coat to dry and then repeat the process with a third colour, covering some of the blocks that have received two coats of paint and some that have received only one, leaving others free of the third coat altogether, to create a pleasing, random effect.*

in your chosen colour and it has dried completely, you are ready to apply the blocks of colour. The pattern you choose to make can be very simple, with just one colour applied over a plain ground, or you can overlap and overprint the colours, as in the second and third steps shown here to create a more mottled effect.

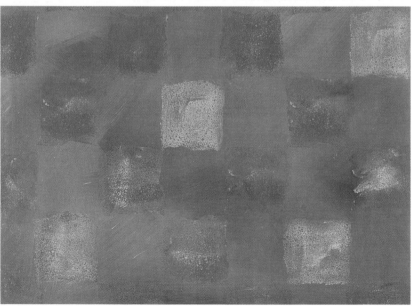

Two variations on the block stamping theme. For the top image the different coloured blocks have been applied in succession. For the image below, the finished surface has been colourwashed lightly afterward to diffuse the printed pattern.

POTATO CUT STAMPING

A very simple way of creating pattern on a painted surface is by means of potato cuts – a return to childhood! It works suprisingly well, provided you keep the design very simple with no difficult corners or edges to rip or blur in the printing. A simple diamond, circle or star motif, for example, can look very professional, with relatively little expertise needed.

You can create the pattern as a border, for example, down the corridor of a hall, as a simple running motif above a skirting board, or as an all-over pattern on the floor, on furniture or on the walls.

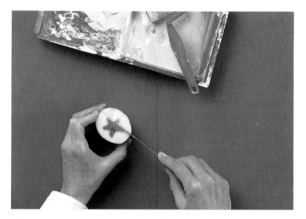

1 Cut a potato in half and then mark the proposed design – a star, as here, or a circle or diamond – with a paintbrush or felt tip. Cut out the design, ensuring that the area stands proud of the rest of the surface by at least half an inch.

2 Using a roller, cover the surface of the pattern with paint and do a couple of test runs on paper, to see how it is working. If necessary, recut any indistinct edges.

3 Apply the stamped design to the painted surface either in a random pattern, as here, in rows, or for a border.

4 Allow to dry, and varnish with several coats of acrylic varnish for any surfaces which will receive a lot of wear.

PAPERING

Above: A selection of different papers in the principal shades of red, green, blue and yellow, showing how pattern and colour combine when similar tones and shades are used.

Opposite: Black and cream is more welcoming than black and white and has been softened here with the addition of Timney Fowler cushions on the antiqued bench, the narrow black and cream stripes provide a suitably classical back-drop, an effect reinforced by stone urns.

Papering today is a lot easier than it was in days gone by, as the products have been designed with the home decorator in mind, but it still requires a certain amount of technical expertise and ability.

If you have never papered a room before, the hallway is not the best place to start because you are dealing with awkward, high spaces and a large area. Do practise on a smaller room first, to make sure you can handle the mechanical aspects of the job with some confidence.

Firstly, make sure you choose a suitable paper, and not one that is so flimsy it tears easily. Some of the heavier papers are also dificult to apply, so try to choose one that is of good quality and medium weight. Avoid patterned papers with large repeats or with awkward patterns that are difficult to match up successfully, as there will be many angles and corners to negotiate.

You must organize your materials well, so that you have everything you need ready to hand. The paper should be applied to the wall carefully and systematically. Take your time, so that the job is done properly. In a hallway, with constant through traffic, you will have to arrange times when you can be left in peace to get on with the job.

You will need stepladders and planks to cope with the higher parts of the landing. You will probably find the job a lot easier if you use a self-adhesive paper, since you will then not need a pasting table which will occupy half the available space in the hall. With such papers, you simply peel off the backing strip and the paper is ready to hang. Papering is much easier if two people share the work, so one can prepare the paper while the other hangs it.

You can, if you wish, paper your walls with old newspaper or brown wrapping paper – the latter has become fashionable in recent times – but ideally the paper should be suitable for the job in hand. In a hallway or stairwell, the paper is going to receive quite a lot of wear and tear from the frequent passage of people and objects close to it. Since there is little else in the way of decoration, the same rules apply with papering as they do with paint: make the most of the surface area to create visual interest. There is a wealth of choice available to you, not only in pattern and colour, but also in

BASIC PAPERING

Your first task is to estimate the amount of paper you are going to need for the job, so you will have to measure the relevant area and then calculate how many rolls it will take. You can do this yourself by dividing the area each roll will cover into the overall square footage of the space to be papered, or you can, quite simply, ask the assistant in the wallpaper shop to do this for you. The latter is infinitely easier, and you will also be able to ask for advice on how much extra to allow for any repeat patterns. Remember that you will need to allow a small amount (roughly 10cm/4in) extra for each length of paper pasted to the wall to allow for cutting. Remember, too, that you may make mistakes and tear the odd sheet, so allow for that as well. An extra roll surplus to your requirements is probably the best solution. Most shops will allow you to take back any unopened rolls.

WORKING ORDER
It is best to start from the central part of the space when papering a hallway then work back to the front door, then up the stairs to the landing.

HANGING THE PAPER
Pin or otherwise fix a plumbline to the wall at the point at which you are going to start hanging the paper. Then cut the first sheet of paper to length, allowing a surplus of 5cm/2in at the top and bottom. Paste or soak the paper as required by the manufacturer's instructions, or simply peel off the backing strip if it is self-adhesive, fold it into a loose concertina, base down first, with the top edge free. Then carry it up the ladder to the top of the area from which it is to hang. Fix it in position with 5cm/2in to spare at the top, smooth it flat to the wall with a brush, brushing sideways and downwards from the centre of the sheet. When the paper is firmly attached, with no air bubbles, press the top edge into the join with the ceiling or picture-rail so it creases the paper at the join, then cut off neatly with sharp scissors. Press the paper back into position, then repeat the procedure at the foot of the paper. Take a second sheet of paper and match the pattern to the first, hang so that the edges butt up neatly, and repeat the procedure. Use a seam roller if necessary to ensure that the edges stay stuck down. Smooth out any air bubbles working outwards from the centre to the edges with a clean cloth.

NEGOTIATING AWKWARD CORNERS
When you are papering around difficult corners, you will have to adapt the same technique that is discussed above to deal with them. Remember it is always easier to use much more paper than generally needed and to cut back as necessary. It will also avoid any chance of creating a really nasty mess by having to add odd pieces at a later stage.

HANGING STRAIGHT DROPS

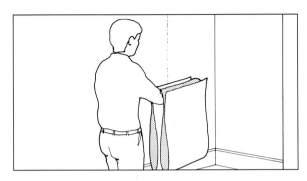

1 *Use a plumbline to draw a vertical line form which you can hang your first drop. Carry the pasted paper folded to avoid creasing it and carry up the stepladder.*

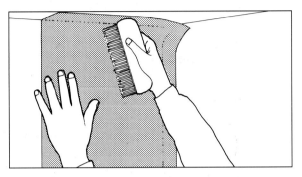

2 *Unfold the top half of the paper and align the edge to the drawn vertical line, allowing an overlap at the ceiling and adjoining wall. To avoid creases brush the paper onto the wall.*

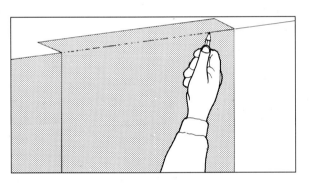

3 *climb down the ladder and unfold the bottom half of the drop and brush over as before. Mark a pencil line along the overlap at the top but don't press too hard as the paper tears when it is damp.*

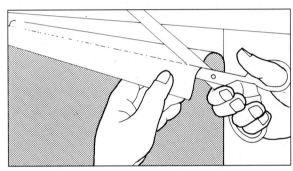

4 *Gently peel the paper back and cut along the pencil mark with long-bladed scissors. Repeat for all overlaps.*

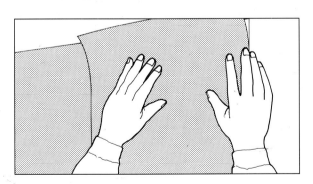

5 *Butt the edge of the second drop against the first and repeat the process as for the first drop.*

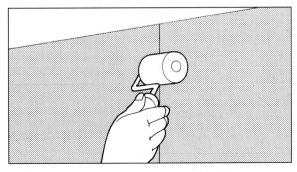

6 *Use a seam foller to go over the jooins to make sure they stick. If extra paste is needed for the seams applyu it with a cheap artists paintbrush*

the textures and weights of papers, as well as the actual finish.

The most expensive papers are those which have been hand-printed. They tend to be delicate and difficult to hang and, in an area like a hallway, they would not be the most suitable choice. You could, however, easily use them as part of a decorative scheme where they could form decorative panels surrounded by larger expanses of cheaper paper or even paint. All other printed papers are machine-printed and are supplied in rolls. The standard roll is normally l0.5m x 53 cm and will have a batch number stamped on it. It is important to buy rolls with the same batch number to ensure that the colour match is identical. Different batches may well have quite considerable variations.

TYPES OF PAPER

The most common wallpapers are non-coated and are not washable; some, however, are coated with PVA (polyvinylacetate) to allow you to wipe them clean with a damp sponge. Vinyl wall-coverings are tougher, and consist of a paper or cotton backing coated with a layer of vinyl on to which the design has been printed. They are often supplied ready-pasted, so that all you have to do is soak them before hanging.

Various alternatives to these traditional paper types can be found. Flock wall-covering, for instance, consists of synthetic or natural fibres stuck to a paper backing to create a raised, textural effect similar to cut pile fabric. Foil wall-coverings have a metallicized plastic film coated over the paper so that they have a very shiny appearance. Paper-backed hessian can be applied like ordinary wallpaper, and you can also use felt and imitation suede but, in hanging these, the wall should be pasted rather than the covering.

Much heavier, textured paper, known as relief or embossed paper, is made from two sheets of paper pressed through a roller and is consequently thick and very durable. It is usually supplied in white, to be painted over, and is ideal for covering the area up to the dado rail, which receives the most wear. These papers were very popular for hallways in Victorian times and have recently come back into fashion. They were manufactured under various trade names, including Lincrusta, which has a raised pattern made from a solid film of linseed oil and fillers fused on to a backing paper.

Other types include thin lining paper, used as the name implies, to cover imperfections in a plastered wall and then painted over or papered over with a better quality paper, and woodchip paper, which

PAINTING AND PAPERING STAIRWELLS

To paint or paper a stairwell, you will need to construct some kind of safe support on which to stand while painting the higher areas. The best solution is to make a scaffolding platform from a couple of pairs of ladders and some stout planks. You will need to put one set of stepladders on the landing area, and then lean an ordinary straight ladder against the wall over the stairwell. Slide the planks through to rest on the steps of both sets of ladders (as shown). Do not allow the span of the plank to be greater than 5ft (1.2m) or it may bend and collapse under your weight.

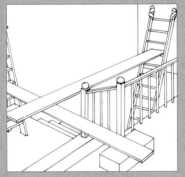

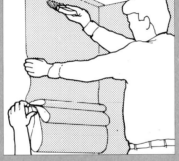

1 *You will need ladders, scaffold boards and a box or hop-up. Lash them together as shown and pad the ends of the ladders to protect the walls.*

2 *Start with the longest drop and recruit an extra pair of hands to help support the folded paper to prevent it from tearing. Repeat the process for hanging straight drops on page 73.*

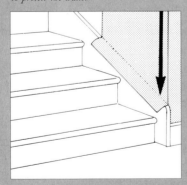

3 *When measuring each drop always use the longest drop at the edge of the skirting and allow for any overlaps.*

is rough-textured and fairly tough and intended for overpainting.

Nowadays, most manufacturers also supply a range of borders and friezes in various widths and colourways to go with their paper ranges. They are applied in the same way as the paper they are destined to match and can be used at cornice, picture rail, dado or skirting height, or to outline any panel or alcove, or even as a door or window surround.

In addition to borders and friezes, you can now also buy paper *trompe l'oeil* decorations which can be used decoratively for various effects from swags and tails to rosettes, bows, knots and even cherubs. They are most frequently used for surrounding a panel, a painting or a window. They are applied in the same way as ordinary papers, but will require careful measuring and positioning, since they form a prominent feature. Make sure that, if you use a succession of them, you line them up exactly and measure the wall in advance to determine their position at evenly spaced intervals.

PAPERING STAIRWELLS

Stairwells present particular problems when papering, as access is tricky and the long drops involved can be difficult to accommodate without tearing the paper. You will have to make a special working platform as for painting and you will need a helper who can support the concertina-like folds of paper while you hang it. Hang the longest drop of paper first, then work around the stairwell, finishing with the head wall of the stairwell. As you go, you will have to measure each drop specially, because it will be shorter than the last. Remember to measure to the longest point of the drop, removing any surplus afterwards.

PAPERING AROUND DOORS

When papering around a doorway, hang the drop immediately before the doorway, and then hang the next one over the opening without pushing it into the frame edge. Trim the surplus paper away to within about l in of the outer edge of the door frame. Cut a diagonal line up into the corner of the door frame, and push the paper back against the wall and brush it into place. Score along the overlap using the edge of the scissor blade, peel away the paper and cut off the excess.

PAPERING AROUND A WINDOW

Treat a flush window in the same way as a door frame, above, but in the case of a recessed window, proceed with the overlapping panel as for the door, then cut into the recess and turn the paper around on to the side reveal. Score and trim it around the window frame in the same way as for the door frame.

PAPERING ARCHES

Paper the outside of the archway as you would a doorway, but allow a margin of lino or so to overlap the edge of the arch. Snip this at intervals, so that the paper will lie flat and fold the flaps back on to the underside of the arch. Paper the inside of the arch with a similar overlap, also folded back on to the underside of the arch. Then cut a strip of paper to fit the width of the arch, but very slightly narrower at the foot and continue around the arch.

PAPERING CUPBOARDS

Parts of rolls can be used to line cupboards or to paper door panels. You can even create fake door panels by fixing wooden mouldings to the surface and papering inside the panelled area. If the door has previously been painted, you will have to remove the paint in order to get the paper to stick, using chemical stripper. Cut the paper to size, but with a narrow border all around of about half an inch. Paste the paper to the panel in the usual way, allowing it to overlap. Then score the panel edge using the blade of the scissor, peel back and trim neatly to the correct size. You can also use left-over paper for random découpage effects, cutting out parts of the paper carefully to make interesting decorative touches. You will need to stick these pieces down carefully, to ensure that the edges do not curl or peel. Varnishing afterwards with matt acrylic varnish should prevent this from occurring.

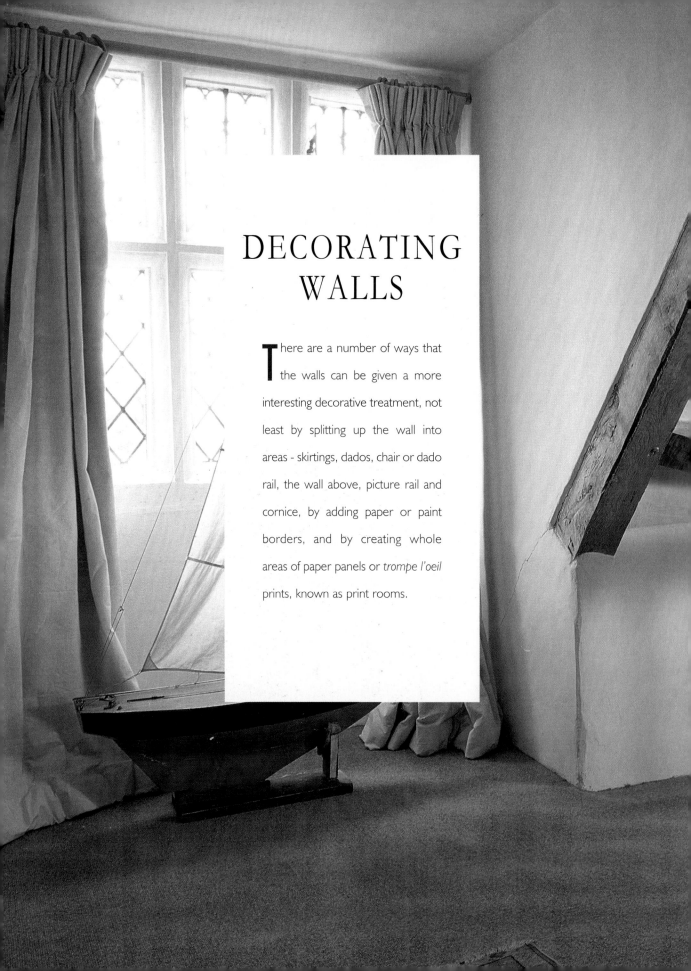

DECORATING
WALLS

There are a number of ways that the walls can be given a more interesting decorative treatment, not least by splitting up the wall into areas - skirtings, dados, chair or dado rail, the wall above, picture rail and cornice, by adding paper or paint borders, and by creating whole areas of paper panels or *trompe l'oeil* prints, known as print rooms.

Decorating walls

You can opt for a range of finishes on the walls, but you must remember that this particular area of the house is going to receive a lot of hard wear, so the surface must be durable. It should not tear or peel easily, if papered, and if painted, it should ideally be wipeable, especially if you have a young family in the house, or dogs. The latter are adept at shaking themselves as soon as they come in through the door, leaving an interesting mud-coloured, spattered effect on the walls. Since young children are likely to use the walls to steady themselves when going up and down stairs, consider painting or papering the dado area in a darker, washable surface. Some of the embossed vinyl papers are very good for this purpose, and so is any painted finish either in gloss paint or matt varnish.

One aesthetic problem with hallways and landings is that very high spaces over a limited area can look oppressive. If this is the case, divide the wall area up with dados, picture-rails or borders (papered or stencilled), or pattern the area in some way to break up the uniformity.

If the area is architecturally interesting, with attractive angles and shapes, then paint it all one colour, or perhaps use tones of the same colour to enhance the chiaroscuro effect and increase the drama. If you use pattern on an area with many different angles, it will be very difficult to paper well and the crossing sight-lines will confuse and distract the eye. In this situation, use the same basic hue for walls and doors, to give the area uniformity. If you look at the photographs of the narrow entrance (page 8) you will see that it gains a great deal in coherence and in spaciousness from the use of a single colourway.

Colour

You have lots of choice when it comes to choosing colour schemes in these common parts, because you rarely have to worry about coordinating the colour with other elements of the room, as you do in bedrooms and living-rooms for example. This leaves you free to experiment with more unusual and more exciting colour schemes.

Remember that dark colours will help to reduce the apparent space and light colours will increase it. Use these attributes to mag-

Previous page: Where there are a number of different planes and angles, as in this loft landing, it pays to stick to a neutral scheme, so that attention focuses on the architectural detailing - the sloping ceilings, exposed timbers and antique bannisters of this landing area.

nify or reduce the architectural proportions of the space.

Splitting the wall area into different colours with, say, a deep blue dado area, a white rail and a white wall with a dark blue stamped fleur-de-lys pattern, will help break up the expanse. On the whole, if you are dividing the walls in this way, keep the deeper colours for the lower levels, both for the reasons of practicality outlined above and to 'ground' the appearance of the area. It does sometimes work to use a lighter colour for the dado area and a deeper colour above, but such a scheme would almost certainly need to have the paler colour repeated above the picture rail and on the ceiling to produce a balanced effect. If you are incorporating a border or a dado rail for the first time, you will need to be careful about matching the angles as it runs from the hall up the stairs and into the landing area. If you intend to have this in the hall you are more or less obliged to continue it through the whole staircase and landing area as well, so do plan the scheme properly from the beginning.

Left: *A long hallway has been given a unifying treatment in butter yellow, burgundy and white. The woodwork has been picked out in yellow, and the low dado papered in an unusual dark-red and white spotted paper.*

DADO AREAS

The ways in which you deal with the lower half of the wall in hall-ways are determined by the effect you are trying to achieve. It was once common to create a panel of matchboarding – strips of tongue and groove timber – from the floor to about 90cm/3ft up the wall. This was done in part to conceal the effects of rising damp, which was prevalent before damp proof courses were introduced, and partly to protect the plasterwork. Unfortunately, the effect of covering the wall with wood was to increase the problems caused by the dampness, encouraging rot. This fashion eventually declined and it became more usual to have a skirting board and sometimes a chair or dado rail, roughly 90cm/3ft from the floor.

If you wish to panel your walls, this can be done quite easily and this is now unlikely to cause any problems with dampness in a

Opposite: Although dado areas are usually associated with an old fashioned Victorian look, the black dado area in this Charles Rennie Mackintosh-style hall proves that they can make a strong, individual statement in any setting.

Right: This subtle combination for dado and wall makes the split between the two areas less obvious by keeping the background colour the same and simply adding pattern to the wall surface in a stylized flower and fleur-de-lys printed paper. The same effect could be achieved with stamping or stencilling. A fine gold border delineates the dado rail.

house provided with a damp-proof membrane. The tongue and groove boarding is nailed to a thin batten fixed to the wall top and bottom and finished at the top with a decorative rail or edging. You can stain or paint the panelling using any of the techniques discussed on pages 117 and on pages 41 to 43. The pre-cut panels match edge to edge, so there is no need for pattern matching, and therefore no wastage.

PAINTING DADOS

It pays to apply the darker paint colours to the area below the dado rail and keep the lighter colours above. You can use a toning or contrasting colour for the dado rail, depending on the choice of colours for the walls. Be careful not to make the dado too dark – it will split the wall too obviously into two separate areas.

Alternatively, if you want to create a durable finish for the lower part of the wall, you can paper it with a heavy-duty

Below: Three different ways to divide up the wall space into dado area, chair rail and the wall above.

Block stamping in sage, terracotta and ochre for the dado area, with ochre colourwashed walls above, separated by an ochre dado rail.

Deep rust and sage combed dado area, with leaf stencilled colourwashed walls above and gilded sage dado rail.

Frottaged dado in ochre, sage and terracotta, with yellow colourwashed walls above and deep blue dado rail.

embossed paper like Lincrusta. This is supplied specially for dado areas in flat pieces, rather than rolls, with either a 90cm/3ft drop or a 100cm/3ft 6in drop. The panels must be fixed with special adhesive, according to the manufacturer's instructions. If you are planning to extend the paper up the stairwell, the panels will have to be carefully organized to cope with the slant created by the need to match the slope of the stairwell.

You can then paint the panels with an oil-based paint or you can antique and distress them (see page 112-115) to give a naturally aged look to the dado area.

PAPERING AND PAINTING DADOS

For hallways, stairwells and landings, a combined decorative scheme of paper and paint can be effective. By and large, the stronger colour is better suited to the area below the dado, where most wear will occur.

Below: A combination of paper and paint has been used to divide the wall spaces shown here.

A green, William Morris-inspired paper covers the dado, while colourwashing in ochre and terracotta over white has been applied to the upper surface, the dado rail is painted in deep burgundy.

Deep blue has been used for the colourwashed dado here, with a cream-based, burgundy-printed paper above and matching burgundy chair rail.

Colourwashing (see pages 58-59) in terracotta is the technique used to decorate the dado area, while a small terracotta print on a cream base covers the area above; the dado rail itself is painted in contrasting deep blue, with an antiqued finish.

Borders and friezes

Borders and friezes have become very popular again, both for finishing off a papered wall and for applying on their own to a painted one to add extra pattern and interest. There is now a huge range of paper borders available on the market, from narrow ribbon-like bands to wide, Victorian-style elaborate friezes. The choice is yours.

They can be used in a variety of ways, but most commonly at chair rail height – normally about 1m/3ft from the floor – and at picture rail or cornice height. Beware of using too many or of making the effect seem too contrived. Borders and friezes tend to look best when used with some discretion, and a very strong colour or obvious pattern will attract an unwarranted amount of attention. They are most effective when used to pick up and echo a colour theme from the rest of the paper or from the floor, thus blending harmoniously with the existing decoration scheme while adding an interesting finishing touch. You are not obliged to use paper – you could create a border with paint instead – but the principle is the same in each case.

Opposite: An unusual cord border has been added just below the cornice in this hall cloak area above newsprint papered walls. The Roman blind has been given a novel surrounding border by using the same pattern on the diagonal - an idea you could copy, using wallpaper for a border.

Right: This cream and terracotta scheme has taken its theme from the kilim hung as a curtain at the window. Cream walls have been made more dramatic with a deep sand-coloured dado rail with terracotta border above.

As with wallpaper, borders come in three different types: self-adhesive, ready-pasted and requiring pasting. If you are pasting your own, proceed exactly as for the main wallpaper. The most important consideration in applying borders is getting them straight, and the easiest way to do this is to use a spirit-level to mark a pencil line on the wall to provide a guide. You will have to make sure that you create neat corners wherever horizontal and vertical strips of border meet.

Paper borders can also be used to make surrounds for doors, for example, or to create a frame for a picture. In a long, rather boring hallway, they can provide a useful decorative link when taken at chair rail height along the wall and then around and above the architrave of each door. You could create an additional feature by adding a decoupage bow, or similar device, at the spot where the vertical and horizontal borders meet at the corners of the architrave. This kind of decorative device helps to unify a hallway which has several doorways opening from it.

Above: A subtly stencilled border defines the cornice area of this landing, the walls are painted to achieve a stone effect. The stencilled border picks up the deep Indian red of the bed coverings.

Right: This deep Aubrey Beardsley-style frieze makes an interesting addition to a landing corridor. A further touch is the gilded surround to the door panels.

PRINT ROOMS

The hall can also be turned into a modern version of the eighteenth-century print room. At the time they were most fashionable they were used to display souvenirs of the Grand Tour. Aquatints and etchings, rather than being framed, were applied direct to the wall and further embellished with applied paper tassels, cords and surrounds. You could achieve a similar effect, using the découpage technique and modern day technology in the form of a photocopying machine.

For your source material for the prints, go to one of the books of collections of Victorian black-and-white prints, such as those produced by Dover, which are copyright free. You can then enlarge or reproduce the images on a photocopier to achieve the size and proportions you require. You will have to sketch out a plan of the arranged prints, to ensure that they fit well together. The ideal position might be an alcove in the hall – for example, a recess under the stairs which has a defined edge – as it will then make a suitable framed area for the mini exhibition.

To achieve a professional finish, it is important that you first cut around the images extremely carefully, using a paper guillotine to ensure straight lines if cutting around rectangular prints, and a scalpel if cutting out curved shapes. The surface to which the paper is glued must be clean, flat, and dust-free, so the plasterwork must be smooth and even, without any bumps or lumps to distort or buckle the images. The images will have to be glued carefully to the wall – simple paper glue works best – and any surplus glue wiped off while still wet. You can also hand-tint the images, using watercolours, gouache, or even coffee, to create a subtly coloured effect. Varnishing afterwards with a matt acrylic varnish will help to protect the prints and flatten any obvious edges.

Creating a professional finish takes patience and time, so make sure you tailor your ideas to suit the time you have available. One solution is to limit the area of the print room to, perhaps, an alcove or one short area of wall between two doorways. You could repeat the border pattern, perhaps, over doorways as an additional detail.

Above: Print rooms have become extremely fashionable again, most frequently using black and white prints, perhaps tinted with a sepia wash, on a deeper coloured ground - yellow, in this case.

CREATING A PRINT ROOM

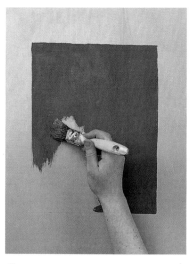

1 *Enlarge the images you need, including the border pattern, on a photocopier with a zoom mechanism, and then hand-tint the photocopies to the colour required – strong coffee makes a good antique pale brown, as used here.*

2 *Cut out the print and trim the border to the size required, using a straight edge and scalpel. You can piece together the border, if necessary, simply matching lengths of repeating pattern, until you eventually achieve the size you want.*

3 *Measure out the area you need for the trompe l'oeil mount, and mark in pencil. Then paint the background colour – a terracotta in this case – and allow to dry.*

4 *Piece together the border and stick in position around the outer edges of the terracotta mount.*

5 *Position the print carefully over the terracotta background, and glue into place with paper glue, smoothing carefully to avoid any wrinkles.*

6 *When completely dry, varnish with matt acrylic varnish. Repeat the procedure at intervals to create the print room, varying the print sizes and the colours of the mounts.*

DECORATING FLOORS AND STAIRS

This section outlines decorative treatments for the floors and staircases, including painting, staining, and antiquing and distressing. The choice will depend to some extent on the condition of both: those with some natural attributes can have these exposed, by staining, colour-washing, liming or antiquing. Those with fewer inherent virtues may need to be covered.

FLOOR TREATMENTS

The floor of any hallway, landing or staircase, without doubt, is going to receive the heaviest wear of any part of the house. It is absolutely essential to make sure that the surface you adopt for it is capable of withstanding this wear. Good-quality flooring is often expensive, but it is money well spent. Make sure that, whatever surface you decide upon, it suits your particular needs.

If, for example, you have a house with no back door, the hall floor is going to take a great deal of punishment and needs to be suitably durable; it must also be reasonably easy to keep clean. A light-coloured carpet, in these conditions, would be totally impracticable, but a washable tile floor would fit the bill. Most houses have wooden board floors underneath the existing carpet, and these can always be laid bare and treated, although the condition of some is not always good enough to be exposed, with badly cut planks and large gaps. If the planks are in reasonable condition, a wooden floor is a practical option for many houses, but for an upstairs flat in a converted house rather than a purpose-built block, the noise levels may be unacceptably high.

FLOOR TILES

Tiled floors are eminently suitable for halls, and carpet can then be used for the stairs themselves and continued up to the landing. When choosing the type of tiling, try to ensure that it suits the architecture of the house. Many old houses were laid with brick tiles or stone flags; these were particularly common in old cottages, where they were laid directly on to earth floors. Being porous, they could 'breathe', thus allowing any damp from the subfloor to evaporate.

Nowadays, damp-proof courses are inserted and the porous nature of the flooring is less important, but natural materials still have a wonderfully rich and lively appearance. Both stone and terracotta tiles are ideal for hallways, and look warmer than ceramic tiles. These are also excellent, if sometimes rather chilly looking in cold climates. Brick paviors can also be used to provide a rich russet-red floor covering that suits most contemporary styles of décor.

Opposite: This cool monochrome treatment with its marble floor tiles is an ideal solution for an apartment hallway, for example, where durability and easy cleaning are important considerations.

Many people who like tiles, but prefer a warmer, softer-looking floor covering, opt for cork, rubber or vinyl floor tiles. These are relatively easy to cut and lay and extremely durable, provided you buy good-quality, heavy-duty domestic wear tiles. Cork tiles will require sealing with a matt varnish to provide a waterproof finish. They are not, however, particularly durable and will show signs of wear in time, with scuff marks and staining if they get very wet. You are likely to find that the area closest to the front door darkens and stains and you may have to replace some of the tiles. It is worth buying more than you need for just this kind of restoration job.

WOOD STRIP FLOORS

If you want a wood floor, but the existing floor timbers are not in sufficiently good condition, you can lay a new strip wood or parquet floor over the top of the existing floor, 'floated' on top of it. There are many different types, styles and patterns, from thin wood strips to chequerboard parquet, sold in squares, and there is a wide variety of wood finishes and colours available. Most of them will need finishing with a varnish or wax sealant before use.

The type of wood will determine the colour and texture of the finish, from deep brownish-red mahogany to light maple wood or pine. You can colour these with some of the new woodstains on the market for an attractive finish, provided they are sold in their natural, untreated condition.

CARPETS AND RUGS

If you opt for fitted carpet, make sure you pick the best you can afford. Stairs in particular are subjected to very heavy wear, and it is important that the carpet you pick is of heavy domestic quality, and fitted with proper underlay. Light colours, while attractive, are certainly going to show any marks. Natural jute and sisal carpets are a popular choice, and are very hardwearing.

Rugs and runners of various descriptions are ideal for hallways, bringing colour and warmth to a hard surface, such as wood, ceramic tiles or stone floors. Rugs on slippery surfaces can be dangerous, however, if you do not fix an underlay to prevent them slipping.

There is a wide choice of styles available, with some excellent cotton dhurries and kilims from the Middle and Far East in a whole range of styles and patterns. Other possibilities are the cotton rag rugs popular in both Scandinavia and North America and

Above: Dark-oak wood stain, or dark paint, can successfully be used for floors, particularly if contrasted with pale walls and woodwork to lighten the overall effect.

Opposite: In this wooden house, paint has been used to brilliant effect by creating delicate variations of hue - shades of yellow, blue and green with similar tonal values - on woodwork and floors. By varying the colour, but keeping the tone the same, uniformity is created without monotony.

the various handwoven rugs with ethnic prints from South America and Mexico.

More expensive versions can be found in the woollen and silk rugs of India and what was formerly Persia (now Iran). Be warned, however, that the hallway will get a lot of heavy use and, although these rugs are all extremely hardwearing, it would be a shame to allow an extremely valuable rug to be spoiled or damaged from overuse. If you do own a valuable old rug or carpet, consider using it as a wall-hanging instead.

Modern rug designers and makers will also produce rugs to order; this can be particularly useful if you have an awkwardly shaped hallway to cater for.

Finally, if you wish, you can paint your own rug, known as a floorcloth, on a cork-tiled or wooden floor. It is not particularly difficult to do, provided you keep the pattern relatively simple. You can use one of the range of new woodstains now on the market, which are ideal for the purpose, or you can use traditional paints if you prefer.

WOODEN FLOORS

If you are lucky, your house or apartment may have an existing wooden floor in reasonably good condition, which you can then renovate to give it an attractive finish. The key elements to look for are sound wooden timbers, without wide gaps between the boards. You can always fill the gaps with fillets of wood, but you might then be better off opting for a different kind of surface.

If the wood is sound, but painted or unattractively stained, you can strip the old paint or stain off using an industrial sanding machine, hired for the purpose. You normally sand the floor with a fairly heavy grade sandpaper wrapped around the drum, then repeat the procedure with finer sandpaper, and sand corners and awkward spaces with a hand-sander. Finally you will have to seal the floor, normally with a matt or glossy varnish, which will require several coats to produce a hardwearing finish. The final colour of the boards will depend on the type of wood and whether you have applied a clear, colourless varnish or a stained varnish.

You can, of course, colour your own varnish if you wish, by adding powder pigment to a colourless varnish. If you add some titanium white to acrylic varnish you can successfully bleach the colour of the floorboards.

Opposite: This elegant tiled effect, with a defining narrow border, has been painted on an ordinary wooden floor. For a hallway, it is imperative to varnish any such effects, using several coats, to make sure it is wearproof.

PAINTING STAIRS

Among the more imaginative solutions to the problems of decorating the staircase is the creation of special paint effects for the stairs and banisters. They are often objects of considerable architectural quality and should be displayed to their greatest advantage. All too often the central part of the treads and risers is carpeted, with a painted surround for the stairs themselves, the banisters and skirting. The different elements here can have a variety of treatments, and you are not obliged to carpet the stairs but in a family house which has a lot of traffic on the stairs, noise could well be a problem if you do not do so.

A popular solution at the present time is to use toning paint effects to create a greater sense of depth and architectural structure. This technique can be used successfully in the staircase area with several toning shades of one colour. Specialist paint companies produce attractive ranges of paints with subtle differences of tone in the colourways and their catalogues are an ideal tool for helping you to make your choice. You can paint the walls up to dado height in a deep colour – say ochre – with a paler tone of sand above, an off-white dado rail, or a deeper shade of ochre, with the skirtings in a toning deeper sand shade. Then you can paint alternate banister rails in three of the four shades you have chosen to underline this toning effect.

Another possibility is to leave the stairs uncarpeted and to paint the risers and treads in different shades of the same colour, using a deeper shade for the tread and a paler one for the riser and toning shades of the same colour for the banisters and skirting. The walls could then be papered with a pattern that picks up these colours.

Avoid any scheme which is too fussy in this area. The movement and change of form created by the flight of stairs and the carving of the banisters need unity rather than distraction, and the most successful schemes will be plain rather than highly decorative.

Equally, if you are planning to use the staircase area as a small gallery for displaying prints or pictures (see page 128), it pays to keep the colour and decoration scheme simple and unadorned, to provide the best possible setting for the display. Photographs or

Opposite: This boarded stairwell would be easy to copy; it successfully employs two oddly contrasting colours - a deep bottle green and a brighter, more leafy green for the floors and stair treads. If you do not want the antiqued, worn effect, numerous coats of varnish will be needed to make it wearproof.

black-and-white prints, elegantly framed, look particularly good in this kind of setting; white, off-white and yellows of various descriptions make an excellent background for displaying black-and-white images.

If you like to try out various paint effects, you will certainly find plenty of scope in the staircase area for a whole succession of ideas, including stencilled patterns on the stairs themselves. These can be repeated on the risers, taken up in a linked motif up the skirting board, or run along just above the skirting board as a border pattern through from the hall up to the landing.

If you are planning such a scheme, do not be over-ambitious. Pick a stencil pattern that is simple to execute, so that the whole project does not take over your life. A simple geometric motif – perhaps taken from a popular ethnic design source such as African prints – is ideal, as it is quick and relatively easy to execute and does not require great artistic skill. More complicated patterns, incorporating ribbons, fruit and flowers, really require several colours to be stencilled over each other to do them justice; this can turn into a very labour-intensive undertaking over such a large area.

In larger, more formal hallways, marbled paint effects look both classical and convincing, but these do take time to produce properly

DRAGGING

This is done by drawing the brush through a coat of wet glaze, painted over a base coat. The base coat shows through to create the finished effect.

1 Over a base of eggshell (white in this case), apply a coat of scumble glaze, tinted in this case with burnt sienna. In dragging this first glaze is applied in an up-and-down direction only.

2 Using the same brush, working into the wet glaze, go over the surface smoothing out the glaze, working in a vertical up-and-down movement to create an even finish.

and may well be beyond the scope of most amateurs. If you are marbling anything for the first time, stick to a small object, such as a piece of furniture – maybe a marbled container for umbrellas – rather than starting on the entire stairwell. Dragging is a useful technique for the actual paintwork, as it breaks up large areas and makes them less flat-looking and dull. You can, without difficulty, drag the paintwork of the doors, skirtings and staircase and provided you opt for a reasonably subtle combination of closely toning colours laid over each another, diagnose any irregularity in the brushwork.

When dragging any area of paintwork you will first need to apply a base coat a shade or two lighter or darker than the top coat through which you will drag a brush to give the finished effect. You paint the base coat first and allow it to dry. You then mix a watery glaze coat (from either oil-based glaze, which you can buy ready-made or acrylic-based glaze, also bought ready-made and which dries more quickly, but does not have such an attractive sheen) which you then apply in smallish blocks over the base coat. While this is still wet, you drag the brush down vertically from the top of the wet area to the base, leaving just enough wet paint untouched as a margin into which to feather the next block of wet glaze, as shown below.

3 *Using a soft bristled or flogging brush, go over the same area in even vertical movements to create fine vertical lines. Wipe any surplus glaze off the brush between strokes.*

4 *The finished effect should look even and smooth. On larger areas where you may have to stop the dragging movement before a whole vertical line is completed. make sure that you do so at different points on each panel so that there is no waterline mark running across the wall.*

BLEACHING WOOD

A nother option after sanding the floorboards is to bleach them to a paler shade. Most floorboards, except in very old houses, are made of a softwood such as pine, which can turn an unattractive, slightly orangey shade on varnishing. Bleaching removes this orange tone and leaves the boards an attractive whitish-grey brown, which acts as an excellent foil for most modern decorative schemes. An advantage with this kind of finish is that it does not have to look particularly perfect, and you may well be able to get away with a single sanding, reducing time and labour as a result.

The method used to bleach the colour from the boards is known as 'liming'. A certain amount of lime is worked into the boards, bound in a wax-based or water-based paste, which then effectively pales or bleaches the colour of the boards. Once this has been effected, you have to seal the floor to prevent the boards becoming scuffed and dirty. With a wax-based liming paste you

**BLEACHING FLOORS
AND PANELLING**
If you wish to create a pale wood effect, you willl need to strip the surface back to bare wood, rinsing it with vinegar to neutralize the acid if you have used a chemical stripper. Liming is the easiest method of bleaching wood; you will need a tin of liming wax, some fine grade steel wool, and some furniture wax. Stained floors should be varnished or waxed as a final precaution against wear.

1 Strip the wood, if necessary, and seal with a coat of shellac.

2 When the shellac has dried, open up the pores in the wood with a wire brush, to allow the liming paste or wax to adhere to it.

have to use a wax-based sealant, which is not ideal for an area with lots of traffic. The water-based liming paste can have an acrylic-based varnish applied over it to seal it. This finish is generally preferred by most people.

You can also colourwash the floor, liming it to create a pale pastel, bleached effect. Colours commonly used are light greens, greys or blues, which are then limed over the painted coat. The best type of paint to use for this purpose is a water-based acrylic paint or an emulsion as a simple wash of colour over the boards. Once this is dry, you can then lime the boards in the normal way.

WORKING ON FLOORS

Remember when working on any finish for a floor or laying a new floor that you must work from the furthest corner towards the doorway to give yourself an escape route. Plan the work carefully so that, if you are varnishing or painting the floor, you can leave enough time for the surface to dry before it is walked upon. This means at least 24 hours and even then be careful. However if you use an acrylic varnish it will dry very rapidly.

3 Apply the liming paste with fine-grade wire wool, allow to dry for 20 minutes and then buff up with a soft cloth.

4 The finished bleached effect.

COLOURWASHING FLOORS

Another valid option for wood floors is to colourwash them. Much depends on the state of the existing floor. If the boards are new, clean and unvarnished, you could, for example, use one of the new range of woodstains, then varnish the finished effect to make sure it stays clean.

If the floor is old and dirty, you will have to prepare the floor first, which is hard work and time-consuming, but not impossible. You sometimes find the boards have been partially stained or varnished, perhaps where a central strip of carpet has run down the hall and up the stairs, with the outer border darker than the central area. This can be used to your advantage to create an interesting bordered effect.

COLOURWASHING AND LIMING

1 Prepare the wood first, brush on a thin coat of woodwash colour and allow to dry.

2 Apply liming wash with fine-grade steel wool, making sure it is well absorbed into the surface.

3 Allow to dry for about 20 minutes, and then go over it with beeswax and steel wool.

4 Finally buff it up with a soft cloth.

MAKING A FLOORCLOTH

Floorcloths were the prototypes for the linoleum of the forties and fifties, and enjoyed their heyday in the late eighteenth century. They can be used in a wide variety of situations, but are obviously ideal in hallways and landings. You must decide the style of the pattern and the size of the floorcloth at the very beginning. Once finished, it is as hard-wearing as any other recommended heavy-duty domestic surface, and can be wiped clean when required.

There are no limits to the type of pattern and the colourways, but it is a good idea to keep the design in tune with the décor of the rest of the house and with its architectural period. If you consult some of the old household manuals, you will find no shortage of ideas – floorcloths of all descriptions were once extremely popular.

You will need canvas for a traditional floorcloth; this can be purchased from either a yacht chandler's or from an artists' supplier. The lengths can be stitched together if necessary. You will need to prime the surface first with a watered down PVA/emulsion wash, or with acrylic primer, and you can then paint the pattern on the primed surface with emulsion paints or acrylics. A mock floorcloth can be painted or stained directly on to the surface of the wood.

DESIGNING A FLOORCLOTH

You must first decide on the area you wish to cover and the kind of pattern you want to use. The most straightforward design is a repeating stencilled motif set in a border of some kind. To achieve a suitable, regularly spaced pattern you will have to organize a template of the area, so that you can position the stencilled motifs in the right place to achieve a regular pattern. The easiest procedure is to measure the area and then draw it out to scale on a sheet of squared paper, using the centre of the squared paper as the centre-point for the pattern.

To transfer the design to the floor itself, use chalk, string and a straight-edge to work out where the motifs should be placed. You can use a variety of paints or wood stains for the pattern, but if there is any danger of smudging, then go round the outline of the pattern with a scalpel blade to prevent the paint spreading into the surrounding wood. Keep plenty of rags to hand to wipe up any smudges or spills.

Plaid floor runner

This design is ideal for a floor runner in a hall, creating the effect of a floor rug on a painted floor. It could also be used for a traditional floorcloth, executed on canvas.

You will need to use a dense, strong paint, such as one of the new traditional paint types that require only one coat to create an area of solid colour. This particular pattern is done by hand and eye, using a roller and an artist's brush. It is fairly easy to execute and relatively quick to complete. The traditional paints dry quickly, so you do not have to wait long between applying the consecutive coats of paint, but each one must be completely dry to the touch before the next one is applied.

You will need to varnish the painted surface thoroughly once it is completely dry with several coats of acrylic varnish to make the surface completely hard-wearing.

MAKING A PLAID RUNNER
Plan the area to be covered in advance and mark it out in pencil to determine the size of the squares.

1 Paint the base of the area in dark-blue traditional paint. Once this is dry, using a 2in (5cm) wide roller, apply first the horizontal stripe in ochre and, when this is dry, the vertical stripe in grey.

2 Allow to dry, then apply a horizontal Indian red stripe just overlapping the ochre stripe. Allow this to dry, and then, using an artist's brush, apply the fine line of paint just outside each of the vertical stripes, and then each of the horizontal stripes, to complete the pattern. Once this is completed, allow to dry, and varnish with several coats of acrylic varnish.

The finished pattern, approximately 3ft (90cm) in width; if you wish to make a consistently repeating pattern for a larger area, keep the Indian red strip to the same side of the ochre stripe, rather than either side of it, as for this narrower pattern.

PAINTED FLOORS

Hard surfaces can always be painted, giving floors a new lease of life. Provided you varnish the painted surface thoroughly, this kind of surface can be as hard-wearing as any other. It also enables you to choose from a wide range of colours and finishes and is an excellent solution for a less than perfect wooden floor. If you have a limited budget and a really poor-quality floor, you can cover it with hardboard and then apply one of the special paint effects to the resulting surface. You will be surprised how effective this can be, particularly if dressed up with a couple of attractive, washable rugs.

One of the best effects for a painted floor is achieved by the decorative technique known as 'combing', which uses a comb-like tool with rubber teeth to create a basket-weave or honeycomb pattern. In fact, you could use almost any implement to create the pattern.

To get the best effects from combing you will need to treat the surface properly, sanding and priming the base surface first and then

COMBING

This technique is ideal for adding surface interest to, say, a hardboard floor. The pattern you choose will be dictated by the teeth of the tool you use. You can buy purpose-made rubber combs or you could make your own from cardboard. When working into the glaze with the comb, cover areas about 2m (6ft) square so that the glaze does not dry out before you work into it. Varnish the entire surface when dry with several coats of acrylic varnish

1 *Paint the base colour, in this case terracotta eggshell, covering the surface as evenly as possible, and allow to dry.*

2 *Paint a thinner glaze coat over the surface, in this case made of emulsion and acrylic scumble glaze in a toning colour.*

applying a couple of coats of, ideally, an oil-based flat paint to provide the overall cover. Work into the second coat, applied in 1.2m (4ft) squares, the implement of your choice to create the chosen pattern.

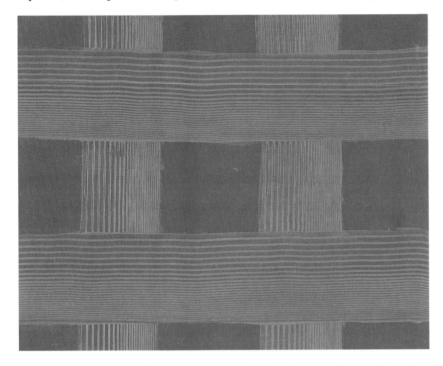

Left: A simple combed pattern in a green glaze over a burgundy base coat.

3 *Draw the comb through the glaze in horizontal bands, a comb's width apart.*

4 *Complete the effect by drawing vertical bands through the glaze.*

ANTIQUING AND DISTRESSING

There are various elements in a hallway which might benefit from antiquing and distressing techniques. You may, for instance, be combining items from a number of periods and, to help the new match the old, you can 'antique' the former. For example, a new door to a cupboard under the stairs can be made to match other doors in the hallway, or a picture frame match an existing old one, or even the hall floor matched to that of an adjoining room. A whole range of techniques is available for this purpose, and the method you use will be determined largely by the finish on the items to be matched.

If you are trying to distress a painted surface, this usually involves rubbing some of the paint back to show more than one layer. This must be done in a sufficiently random manner to look like the result of genuine wear and tear. Look first at any item and note where it receives the most wear – on edges and corners and where it is handled, perhaps around a door knob. These are the areas to concentrate on when rubbing back the top coat of paint.

How far you want to go in this attempt at verisimilitude is up to you, and the amount of time you have at your disposal, but normally a couple of coats of paint and one go at rubbing back will serve the purpose. Occasionally, if you are antiquing a piece of furniture which has a white base coat, for example, you may need to add an extra layer of paint to prevent the white showing through when it is rubbed back.

Another tool used in antiquing is dark wax, which is rubbed into the finished paint effect with steel wool, scoring the paint so that the wax adheres to the cracks, producing an effect of genuinely aged scratches and scuff marks. It also takes the new sheen off the paint. This wax can be bought in a wide range of colours from dirty dark browns to absolutely colourless; what you buy depends on the effect you want to achieve.

Remember that the waxing is the finishing touch, because once you have applied the wax, you cannot paint again over the top without stripping the wax off with white spirit.

Above: The banisters on this landing have been antiqued with a mixture of dark green and raw sienna. When antiquing wood, make sure you rub off the parts that naturally wear - the raised mouldings for example - to give the most realistic finish.

Opposite: This stairwell has been given an antiqued finish by painting several toning coats of paint over a darker brown base, and rubbing back with wire wool to reveal the previous coats of colour. Pale blue or pale grey over brown look particularly effective, as does an ochre over a dark sienna.

Another attractive ageing technique is the rubbing of a little gilt cream along the edges of a frame, say, to recreate the well-worn effect of old gilding. You can buy the cream in different colours in small pots; all you have to do is smear a little along any prominent ridges or edges with your finger. The cream dries hard and will stay in place if not knocked or buffeted. You could gild a chair or picture rail in this way, or perhaps a curtain pole, or indeed any form of decorative moulding, so that the relief elements are picked out and highlighted.

If you want to antique an emulsion wall, you can simply paint a thin, fairly dingy glaze over the surface, rubbing it in well with a rag, and perhaps varying the colour of the glaze in places slightly. You might wish to use this kind of method where you have extended or altered the dimensions of a hallway. A good 'dirtying' glaze is recommended by Althea Wilson in her book *Paint Works*.

STAMPING A DESIGN

For this design, a bought rubber stamp of a pineapple was used, together with traditional water-based paint, and a small 5cm (2in) roller and tray. It is important to do a test run first to see how well the image transfers. When transferring the stamped design on to the wall or floor, give it steady all-round pressure to ensure it transfers evenly. If you are making a repeating pattern, you will need to mark the positions for the stamps first in pencil.

1 Cover the stamp with a thin layer of fairly dry paint (traditional paint is ideal) using a small roller. Make sure the stamp is just covered, and the paint is not too thickly applied. Try a test stamp on a piece of paper first.

ANTIQUING AND STAMPING

You can create a suitably antique look for a stamped design if you pick the colours fairly carefully, and then wash over the design after you have created it using a thin glaze of paint. This type of look is well suited to painted furniture, for example, and could be used to decorate a hall table, perhaps, or a small chest. You could stamp the design directly on to wood, if you wished, rather than a painted surface, and then antique it as for wood using antiquing wax, rubbing it in with fine-grade steel wool.

If you are creating a stamped or stencilled design, rubbing it back will help give it a broken, slightly aged appearance, and can also be used to remove any unsightly blobs of paint inadvertently created in the stamping or stencilling process. Most stamped and stencilled patterns look much more attractive if only partially visible, rather than too uniformly executed, so do not worry if your first attempts are uneven - it adds to the charm.

Above: *The finished stamped pattern after being washed off with a coat of pale glaze.*

2 Apply the stamp to the prepared painted surface, rolling it slightly from side to side in a rocking motion, but without moving it from the spot or it will smudge.

3 When the stamped design is completely dry, apply a thin white glaze (made up of paint and acrylic glaze) as a wash over the area, and then rub this off with a slightly dampened cloth, leaving a pale haze over the painted surface, which will also knock back the colour of the stamp. For a more antique effect on a pale painted surface, colour the glaze slightly with light brown acrylic paint.

115

STAINING A FLOOR

You can use some of the new ready-made woodstains, available from a number of manufacturers, to stain an untreated or sanded floor. They differ from the old woodstains in that they are water- rather than spirit-based, and are much easier and more pleasant to use.

The colours have been created to give the wood just a gentle wash of colour, rather than a strong stain. One of the problems of using the old spirit-based woodstains was that the colour was often too strong and the finished result patchy where the wood took it differently, soaking it up at some points and not at others. The new stains seep into the wood itself and colour it gently, but this does mean that it is not possible to remove it once the work has been done.

The range of colours tends towards soft art shades. Those that work best are the Indian reds, soft sage greens and dusty blues, which have been used as paint effects in Scandinavia over the centuries. The advantage of a woodstain over a painted finish is that it allows the natural grain of the wood to show through, giving the floor an attractively textured finish.

If you want to stain a floor which was formerly painted or varnished, you will need to prepare the surface first. One of the problems of staining stripped rather than new wood is that it may take the stain in patches. To avoid this, you must size the floor first before staining it, using thinned down acrylic varnish if you are going to apply a waterbased stain over the top.

Before staining, you will first need to remove all traces of any existing finish, probably by lightly sanding them. This is a messy, time-consuming job, for which you will probably have to hire a sanding machine, as well as a smaller sander to do edges and corners.

MAKING A DECORATIVE WOODSTAIN PATTERN

You could create a border using differently coloured woodstains quite simply.

First mark out the design – in this case a simple double border – using a straight-edge and a pencil. Then score along the pencil lines with a scalpel to prevent the stains seeping into each other.

Above: Here, an all-over pattern using three different stencils, two large and one small, has been created for a hall corridor, with wooden boards. The stencils are painted a darkish green, but any deep colour – dark blue, grey or red – would be suitable for this kind of effect.

Left: This kitchen shows how pale pine can be antiqued to give a much richer finish, by applying a brown base coat, over-painted with a lighter brown, and then rubbed back in places to reveal the base coat. Varnish when dry.

Secondly, apply masking tape, or hold a card against the pencil line, and apply the wood stain to the first part of the border.

Thirdly, repeat with the second colour for the other part of the border.

Finally, stain the rest of the floor area in the usual way.

ANTIQUED STENCILLED FLOOR

One of the most attractive ways to deal with an old wooden floor, perhaps not in the very best condition, is to make a virtue of necessity, and give it a patterned, antiqued finish. This will help disguise any imperfections in the boards, while adding to the overall character.

For a hallway, you can opt for a simple border pattern in a large

1 Clean the existing wooden floor with white spirit to remove any grease or polish. If you wish, colourwash the floor (see page p.56) to achieve an attractive base colour. In this case, a light Indian red was used over a yellow ochre. Then, using a stencil brush and holding the stencil card with one hand, pounce the chosen colour for the stencil through the stencil card, overlapping the patterns in a random style.

2 Once you have completed the pattern and it has completely dried, you can antique the finish with a dark antiquing wax. Apply it with a soft dry rag, and rub well into the wood. Allow to dry and then buff up.

square hall or a central floor rug-style pattern; in a narrow corridor you might try an all-over stencilled pattern in a loose, overlapping easy-to-work design.

The main aim is to give yourself a design which is loose enough not to require precise measuring and marking, so that you avoid a great deal of pre-planning and can create the design as you go, moving the stencils by eye to the required positions. Overlapping the stencils will help to create this informal look but you will need to choose stencil patterns which adapt well to this kind of design. Curling designs are obviously more suitable than geometric ones, although a simple repeating geometric pattern is easy to execute as a border, for example.

Left: The finished pattern over six boards. It can be used as a repeating pattern over a long hallway or as it stands to mak· an imitation floorcloth.

COMBED AND STENCILLED PATTERN

1 Paint the area with a coat of dark Indian red traditional paint, and allow this to dry. Then apply, very roughly and patchily, a second coat of dark green paint, and allow this to dry, and then rub back with fine-grade wire wool to give an antiqued effect.

2 Apply a broad brush stripe in pale grey glaze to the width of the comb you intend to use and, while it is wet, drag the comb through the wet glaze.

3 Cut out a small diamond stencil in stencil card and, using the same grey but this time in thicker paint, pounce the colour through the stencil with a small stencil brush.

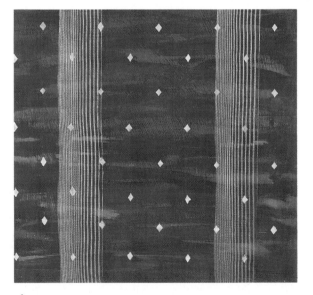

4 When it is dry, apply several coats of acrylic varnish.

PAINTING STAIR TREADS

You can create interesting paint effects on the risers and treads of a staircase. Remember, though, that both will get a lot of hard wear and you will need to create a pattern that will cope with the knocks and scratches. A painted staircase might be a good solution for a loft staircase that has been added later to the house, for example, turning it into a feature in its own right.

As is the case with all floor finishes, any paint effect will need to be well varnished to protect it and to cope with the amount of wear it will receive. The pattern shown here could be used just as successfully for a floor design, or for a dado area if preferred. Combing, the technique used for creating the stripes, is easy to carry out and can be used for chequerboard effects as well. If preferred, these can be used just on the riser, leaving the tread plain.

Left: A Greek key pattern, taking its theme from the frieze at the back of the hall, has been stencilled in ochre on the stair risers, with the stencil motif echoed on the walls, as a border above the skirting and to create panels.

FURNITURE
AND
EFFECTS

Small free-staning items of furniture, pictures, prints and mirrors, as well as drapes and hangings of various descriptions can all help to create an attractive and welcoming atmosphere in hallways and landings. Paint effect techniques can be used to brighten and transform junk shop bargains and clever use of display techniques for pictures, as well as lighting, can create a focal point on a stairwell or end wall, for example.

FURNITURE

Above: An unusual peg-rack makes a sculptural feature in the hallway, against brilliant yellow colourwashed walls. Wrought iron, papier maché or carved wood are often used for similar pictorial motifs for racks of pegs.

Opposite: The understairs area has been opened out to provide a place for an elegant painted bench, the kilim rug and tapestry cushions provide contrasting colour accents.

In most hallways there is relatively little space for furniture, therefore you need to choose carefully when it comes to buying or decorating hall furnishings.

The chief criteria are to do with space and style. If the hallway is narrow, for example, you need furniture which takes up relatively little depth, although you have a little more space for manoeuvre if the understairs area is opened up. Narrow bookshelves and cupboards are always a possibility and there is a range of interesting shapes and storage ideas that you can use in even narrow spaces. For example, there is often an angle in the hallway in which a corner cupboard can be incorporated. These days you can get some quite stylish corner cupboards made up in MFI, as opposed to wood, which is much cheaper and also relatively lightweight. Once painted, it is impossible to tell the difference between MFI and wood, and if you are hanging the cupboard on the wall, then the lighter weight is an advantage.

You can look around for a range of hall tables, some rectangular with a couple of drawers, some semicircular. Some sort of shelf or flat surface is almost essential in a hallway, to give you somewhere to put any mail, or for guests to leave small belongings when they visit the house.

If you have room, try to incorporate some kind of hanging area for guests' clothes. Again, the understairs area is ideal, but failing that you can incorporate attractive wall hanging units, perhaps with a decorated board into which the hooks are inserted. Some of the imported ironware from the Far East is cheap and attractive, with panels of hooks in interesting shapes.

LIGHTING

Lighting is another factor in a hallway. It needs to be bright but soft. Wall lights are ideal, but if you have to make do with hanging bulbs, then try to make sure that the shade diffuses the bulb in some way. Nothing is less welcoming for visitors than to have to face the glare of a bulb which is sometimes of searchlight proportions.

You can, if you have some attractive paintings, light them

individually with a small overhead light. This is the best way to see the painting, and is certainly worth doing if you have invested in any kind of valuable work of art.

Another alternative is to use table lamps in the hall – ideally desk lamps positioned on a small console table. This is infinitely more attractive and more welcoming than overhead lights, unless you have the space and money to put in crystal chandeliers, which give off a similarly bright but diffused light.

Think, too, about how the stairwell itself is lit. It is important to be able to see the stairs clearly in order to avoid accidents, and again a couple of wall lights up the staircase are an ideal solution.

From a pratical point of view, it also pays to have some kind of lighting outside the door, to light the path and the doorstep, both for convenience and for security. There are various lighting devices that are triggered by pressure or a beam, so that they come on only when needed.

Opposite: This large understairs area has been converted into a small study area, while the stairwell above provides useful gallery space for a collection of prints.

Left: This minimalist Twenties landing is an elegant study in form and texture; the off-white walls and central runner on the wooden floorboards help to reflect the light from the window.

127

PICTURES AND PHOTOGRAPHS

A hallway is an ideal place for a collection of pictures, prints or photographs. There is usually plenty of uninterrupted wall space, including the area up the stairwell, which is ideal for housing a large display. If you have small items in a collection – whether toy cars, matchboxes or other similar items – consider combining them on a display shelf.

It is important when arranging any kind of collection on the walls to theme it in some way so that it provides an attractive overall image, rather than a series of disparate pieces. If the pictures are of various sizes, with different kinds of frames, then try to put them together in a way that makes some kind of composition. It will help if the pictures, prints or photographs can have some similarity of framing – whether clipped glass or wooden frames. Mixing the two tends to look bitty and unattractive. Alternatively, separate the two areas out, putting the clipped glass frames together in one group, and the wooden frames together in another.

Where and how you hang pictures depends to some extent on the organization of the area, but try to group them where they can be seen to best advantage, in the best light. If you have a hall table half way down the hall, then group the pictures around and above the table, in a large block of images. Do not scatter them piecemeal around the walls, in the hope that it will help give the whole area interest. They will simply lose impact, unless the items are particularly large, and if they are, a hallway is probably not the best place to hang them, since you can never get far enough back from the image to get a proper look at it as a whole. Smaller items suit this kind of space much better.

Think carefully about the height at which you hang the pictures. If you are displaying a large group of them you can position the top ones higher than normal, but in general pictures look better if hung at eye level, or thereabouts. They can look very uncomfortable if positioned too high, making the onlooker feel dwarfed in comparison. If you have two doorways in the hall, position the collection of pictures, or a single picture, midway between them. It will jar if it is positioned off-centre.

Left: *The height of most stairwells gives you the perfect display area for larger than normal prints or posters, while the window sill provides a display shelf for a collection of animals. Creating a theme - in this case of wildlife - helps to add unity to the look.*

When hanging pictures, it is important that the hooks are secure and strong enough to hold the weight and that the picture hooks are positioned in exactly the right place. Ideally, you need someone to help you, but if you are putting up a collection of pictures, you could try laying them out first on the floor or on a table, to decide how you wish to display them. Pictures are often of disparate sizes, and you will have to make a judgement as to which elements of the frame to line up – the tops or bottoms or the sides. Experiment with different formations until you find one that you think does justice to the pictures, and looks good as an entire compositon.

Another, much simpler collection of art for the hall can be your own children's paintings or drawings. Since this may well change as time goes on, it probably pays to devote a framed section of the wall to their efforts. Cork is an ideal base since you can pin into it very easily, perhaps covered with fabric to make it look less obvious. Green baize would make an ideal covering, perhaps surrounded with decorative brass nailing. You could incorporate the brass nailing as a decorative feature elsewhere in the hall, making imitation panelling with it.

SHELVING AND CUPBOARDS

Another good idea for a hallway is a high shelf at picture rail height on which all sorts of bits and pieces can be collected, perhaps with hooks under for hanging hats and bags. Shelving does not have to be boring, and you can make interesting forms and shapes with the shelves. One hallway could have a hanging shelf with a particularly pretty A-frame shelf displaying a collection of earthenware jugs, while another might have a delicate filigree ironwork set of shelves with small photographs.

Various paint effects can be employed to make shelving more interesting, and you could carry a colour theme for picture rails or dado through to the shelving, for example, so that it tones in with these other areas of paintwork. Paint, again, covers a multitude of sins, including less than attractive shelving materials, and the ubiquitous MFI board comes into its own again. Being narrow, the cheap, chain-store, free-standing shelving is ideal for hallways, and you can combine it in various configurations to suit the space available – tall and narrow or wide and long for example.

FREE-STANDING FURNITURE

Umbrella stands are particularly valuable, and even the heavy Edwardian kind with a back panel can be given a new lease of life with some attractive paint effects to turn it into a special feature. You can sometimes find original Victorian cast iron umbrella stands, which could be given a distressed paint finish in verdigris, for example. Alternatively, a large earthenware or ceramic pot can perform the same function.

Equally good in halls are the old-fashioned Victorian plant stands on which an aspidistra, or castor oil plant, used to stand in its heavily coloured ceramic pot. These can be used for plants, or just for decoration in themselves, but it is certainly welcoming and attractive to have a plant or two, or a flower arrangement in the hall. You need to be a little careful if the hall is very dark, as very few plants, apart from

Above: Umbrella stands are not only useful, they can often be attractive items of furniture in their own right. Cast-iron versions can be painted in interesting colours, and given an aged, distressed appearance.

Opposite: These ingenious built-in cupboards with sliding doors have made excellent use of the area under the stairs in a highly functional and yet aesthetically pleasing manner.

Above: The combination of candle wall lights and a large glass mirror, coupled with the white painted furniture and brilliant sunshine colourwashed walls, floods this hallway with colour and light.

the forementioned aspidistra, survive well without adequate light. Other good stand shapes and ideas include music and shaving stands. The latter would make an attractive addition to a hall cloakroom, for example.

MIRRORS AND GLASS

Mirrors are an obviously valuable addition to any hall, since they help to enlarge the available space via the reflection. Make sure the frame and style is in keeping with the decorative scheme you have in mind. You can often find old mirrors in junk shops which can be given a new lease of life with painting or gilding effects. You could also incorporate a mirror into a corner cupboard door, using old mirror glass. Do not be put off by marks and imperfections in the glass – it is part of the charm. Simply give the cupboard or the frame a similarly aged and distressed finish.

If you are lucky enough to have stained glass in the front door,

Right: Mirrors can be used successfully to reflect views through from landings and hallways into adjoining rooms, increasing the apparent space. It is important that the decoration scheme of rooms off the hall is linked in some way to that of the hall, stairwell or landing.

or in panels alongside it, it is worth taking this as the key to the decorative scheme and using the colours and general theme of the glass as the starting point. You could echo a motif from the stained glass as a stamped or stencilled design on the walls, perhaps, or even on the stair treads, or as a border along a wooden floor. If you do have this kind of feature, then make sure you do not swamp it with unnecessary pattern or colour that clashes with it. The light and interest it provides will be a far more eye-catching focal point if the rest of the scheme is in harmony with it. You can, of course, go the whole hog and recreate an entire Edwardian look in the hall, complete with dark paper, mahogany wooden finishes and wooden framed pictures, but beware of turning your house into something approaching a museum. It seems like an interesting idea, but the novelty does eventually pall and you may start to feel like a prisoner of the past.

Above: White painted walls, ceilings and woodwork, coupled with the effect of a pale polished wood floor, increase the apparent space in this hallway.

DRAPES AND HANGINGS

Most hallways, stairwells and landings have natural light at some point; more often than not, though, the glass through which it passes is frosted or stained to ensure privacy. If that is the case, curtains are not necessary, except for decoration or for warmth. You may prefer to keep the area uncluttered with fabric, but if you do decide that you want a curtain at a landing or stairwell window, then try to turn it into a worthwhile feature, because it will be, by virtue of its position, quite prominent.

If you decide to have hangings in the hall, stairwell or landing area, you need to consider very carefully what style of curtain or blind is appropriate for the situation. You may find it is desirable to keep the curtain within the area of the window embrasure, in which case a blind is probably the best option.

BLINDS

In its original simple form, called a 'pull-up curtain', a blind consisted of a piece of cloth, cut to the size of the window, and pulled up by cords in the centre to create a curved drape. This form is now known as a London blind. A more elaborate form, with double the quantity of fabric in width, and half as long again in length, ruches the fabric into three or four sections, also pulled up by cords. An even more elaborately ruched form, known as a festoon blind, is also quite common.

If you retain a few basic rules in mind, you should be able to create your own style of blind to suit any window. This is not as fanciful as it sounds, since the key element in creating a successful blind is to ensure that its style is appropriate for the proportions of the window. Nothing looks worse than a heavily ruched blind fitted across a short but very wide window. Such a window would look better with two or three Roman blinds, which fold up neatly with the help of stiffened sections pulled up in the usual way on cords.

When choosing fabric for blinds, you need to think carefully about the situation and the purpose. Architectural blinds are best made in fairly stiff, but not thick, fabric. Cotton reps, sailcloths, and calicos work well, as does mattress ticking. On the whole,

Opposite: This stunning dining-hall makes unusual use of architectural features and of fabric, creating a wonderfully rich contrast of stark wrought iron and rainbow cloth.

plain fabrics look better, although geometric designs such as stripes and checks work well too. Heavily patterned fabrics do not work well; the pattern tends to conflict with the style of the blind. If you want to make sheer blinds instead of the ubiquitous curtains, you can make simple London blinds, which roll up softly at the base but incorporate no extra gathers or frills.

The heading support can also be varied; there is nothing to stop you using an attractively hand painted pole, perhaps with the addition of decorative finials.

Borders and edgings of various kinds can be incorporated successfully. An otherwise plain blind can be enlivened by a contrasting border at the base, perhaps shaped or scalloped.

***Right:** This open-plan hallway turns a high wall into a stunning display area for two brilliant stained-glass style hangings.*

***Opposite:** Hallways and landings provide an excellent area for displaying tapestries and hand-woven hangings, as this Colonial-style hallway demonstrates.*

CURTAINS

You can, of course, create your own curtains too, and again you need to think carefully about the overall shape, since they will occupy a prominent position. If you have a landing with a large window, it is worth creating a generous and gracious treatment for it. Do not forget about the area over the curtain: consider the pelmet as part of the overall scheme. Self-pelmets in the curtain fabric can take a whole range of forms, many of which are easy to make at home. Quilted and padded pelmets, perhaps bordered with a contrasting padded roll of fabric, look good, as do diamond-shape points. Try to ensure that the pelmet and curtain style and fabric match effectively. Do not go overboard on a fashionable curtain design – elaborate swags and tails, for example – if it dwarfs and dominates the whole area and is out of keeping with the furniture and overall scheme.

Grand curtain designs were originally planned for large windows and sumptuous houses. Translated into a typical modern home, the proportions are out of keeping with the architecture and the result looks pretentious and unpleasing. Something more natural, and much simpler, will often work far better.

A single curtain, for instance, hanging from an elegantly distressed pole, with a curtain heading with nice clean lines (simple well-made tabs or hand-sewn pinch pleats) would look much more attractive.

For diversion, you can create some interesting tie-backs for the curtains, so that you can drape them as you wish, or you can border otherwise plain curtains with different braids, rolled and padded borders, or whatever takes your fancy. Even rope can be used as a border or as a tie-back, and can be twisted over the curtain pole itself, perhaps echoing a stencilled rope motif at frieze height.

Another possibility is a half curtain, or cafe-style curtains, hung from the midpoint of the window. Checks and stripes look very good used in this way, but make sure that the curtains are lined and look solid. Flimsy curtains, apart from sheers, look unappealing. If you simply want a sheer curtain, there are some wonderful embroidered voiles and muslins from the Far East, which are inexpensive and much nicer than the ubiquitous nylons and synthetic laces. You are not obliged to opt for the standard track; you can hang them from clips, for example, or simply swathed over a pole.

In a draughty country hallway, a door curtain can be invaluable.

Above: A rich mixture of colours and textures has been used for this mezzanine sleeping area; the walls have been ragged in deep blue, with curtains and chest in cream. Strong contrasts of colours in the ethnic-style cushions and spread provide a glowing feature.

Opposite: An unusual curtain treatment makes a feature of this landing window, with a double curtain in zinging yellow and pink window-pane checks; the front curtain is knotted in the centre.

You will need to use really heavy material, preferably lined and interlined, to act as insulation, and it may also be a good idea to weight the hem to keep the curtain from blowing around when the door opens.

Velvet was traditionally used for such heavy door curtains, and it is still the best option, but if you are using plenty of interlining you can choose the fabric you prefer. A nice idea is to use two patterns, one for the front of the curtain and one for the reverse side, then perhaps

Above: The banister of this landing area provides a place for draping richly coloured kilims, tapestries and quilts to give the area warmth and cosiness.

reverse the borders on each side. A check and stripe look good together, or even a floral pattern and a stripe. If you are mixing patterns, make sure you keep the colour palette similar or with a good connecting link. Deep rich Renaissance colours look good in this kind of setting – golds, reds, greens, purples and deep blues, for example. You can, if you choose, paint the fabric yourself to turn the door curtain into something more interesting and individual, and then use rich braids and tassels to give it a more sumptuous air. Some kind of tieback will be necessary to keep the door curtain out of the way when not in use. Remember that a heavy curtain will need a suitably strong pole or track, well secured to the wall, from which to hang it.

RUGS AND WALL-HANGINGS

Textiles are an unjustly neglected decorative device. In previous centuries, tapestries and hangings were a major form of wall decoration; they also served a functional purpose in keeping out cold and draughts and provided much-needed extra insulation.

Nowadays, although few people have the time to create their own textiles, there is a growing range of attractive dhurries, kilims and tapestries available and the stairwell is an ideal place to hang a large rug , quilt or tapestry and show it off to advantage.

If you are planning to display a large textile in this way, then try to organize the decorative scheme around it. It is going to make a major impact, and you will achieve more satisfactory results if you plan the decoration with its colours and form in mind. You could take just one or perhaps two of the colours it contains as your starting point, or you could perhaps use a decorative feature from it as the inspiration for a stencilled border.

In order to hang the textile in the stairwell area, you will need to construct a working platform to do the hanging, and you will have to choose a suitable method of hanging. You can either use a length of carpet gripper or you can hang the rug from a pole, using a fabric sleeve and hooks. If you are going to use carpet gripper, measure the length required (fractionally shorter than the width of the rug) and saw the gripper to the appropriate length. Remove the floor pins from the gripper, then fix it to the wall with screws, marking a straight horizontal line with a spirit level. You will need to position the gripper on the wall about a quarter of an inch below the top of the rug. Once the gripper is securely fixed to the wall, simply push the rug on to the gripper so that the spikes hold and position the rug. Be careful not to pull or tear the hanging when taking it down for cleaning.

Alternatively, you can hang the rug from a pole suspended between two brackets. The size and weight of the pole will be determined by the weight of the rug, as indeed will be the size of the screws used to fix the brackets to the wall. The easiest method is to make a tube-like fabric sleeve for the pole and slipstitch it to the top of the rug. If you want a less formal hanging, you can use a pole and clips at 10cm (4in) intervals – you can buy decorative clips at most DIY stores.

Above: *The floor of this simple Swedish landing has been made a focus of attention, while the windows have been left bare, simply outlined in the same duck-egg blue as the banisters.*

141

INDEX

UK Sources & Suppliers

It is worth knowing that most of the big paint manufacturers have a customer services department which will help you with queries on materials for different paint finishes, so if in doubt, do consult them. J.H. Radcliffe have been specializing in high quality paints for many years, and will also answer queries. Their tins of glazes, for example, come with an extremely helpful leaflet. Readers not resident in the UK may like to know that all sources listed will supply worldwide via mail order.

L. Cornelissen & Son Ltd
105 Great Russell Street
London WC1B 3LA
Tel: 0171-636 1045
Artists' materials. Pigments. Brushes.
Glazes. Fabric painting materials.

The English Rubber Stamp Co
Sunnydown
Worth Matravers
Dorset BH19 3JP
Tel: 01929 439117

Foxwell and James
57 Farringdon Road
London EC1M 3JH
Tel: 0171-405 0152
Stockists of specialized restoring
materials, including gilding products.

Papers and Paints
4 Park Walk
London SW10 OAD
Tel: 0171-352 8626
Range of specialist paints, plus glazes,
varnishes, brushes and pigments.

Whistler Brushes
(Lewis Ward & Co)
128 Fortune Green Road
London NW6 1DN
Tel: 0171-794 3130

J.W. Bollom & Co Ltd
13 Theobalds Road
London WC1X 8FN
Tel: 0171-242 0313

E. Ploton (Sundries) Ltd
273 Archway Road
London N6 5AA
Tel: 0181-348 0315
All decorating materials for glazing,
stencilling and gilding.

Craig and Rose plc
172 Leith Walk
Edinburgh EH6 5EB
Tel: 0131-554 1131

J.H. Radcliffe & Co
135a Linaker Street
Southport PR8 5DF
Tel: 01704 37999
Brushes, tools and glazes.

Relics
Bridge Street
Witney OX8 6DA
Tel: 01993 704611
All specialist paints, glazes, brushes
and restoration materials as well as
courses in decorative painting taught
by Annie Sloan. Distributors of Annie
Sloan's Traditional Paints.

Simpsons Paints Ltd
122-4 Broadley Street
London NW8 8BB
Tel: 0171-723 6657
Specialists in gold leaf, brushes
and glazes.

Paint Magic
Head Office and enquiries
79 Shepperton Road
Islington N1 3DF
Tel: 0171-354 9696

Polyvine Ltd
Vine House
Rockhampton
Berkeley
Glos GL13 9DT
Tel: 01454 261276
Suppliers of acrylic paint products.

Vargail Ltd
305 Cricklewood Lane
London NW2 2JL
Tel: 0181-455 8660

ACKNOWLEDGEMENTS

The author and publishers would like to thank the following individuals and organisations for their help in putting together this book.

Kate Pollard and Thandi MacPherson for creating paint effects, Emily Hedges for picture research, Michael Crockett and Geoff Dann for photography, The English Rubber Stamp Company for supplying stamps and Laura Ashley for supplying wallpaper samples, Annie Sloan's Traditional Paints were used for the step-by-step photographs.

Picture Credits

Special Photography: **Mike Crockett, Geoff Dann, Susannah Price**

The publisher should like to thank the following sources for providing the photographs for this book:

Abode 5, 9 top left, 17, 26 top right, 27 left, 61, 82, 125, 128, 140

Camera Press Ltd. 32, 33, 122-123, /Peo Eriksson 27 right

Michael Freeman 10-11, 28, 29, 116

Robert Harding Picture Library 124, 129, 132 top left, 133, 138, **/IPC/David Parmitter** 87, **/IPC/Paul Ryan** 40, **/IPC/Fritz von der Schulenburg** 15, **/IPC/Andreas von Einsiedel** 12

International Interiors/Paul Ryan Front jacket (designers: J&S Fell-Clarke), 9 bottom right, 14, 16, 23, 25, 30 top left and bottom right, 71, 81, 83, 88 top left and bottom right, 92-93, 95, 127, 141

Lu Jeffery Back jacket inset right, 57, 136, 139

Marianne Majerus Back jacket and 7 (designer: John Mixer), 8 (designer: Leon Krier)

Ianthe Ruthven Back jacket inset left, 2-3, 18, 19, 31, 49, 78-79, 91, 96, 99, 101, 112, 113, 134

Elizabeth Whiting & Associates 4, 21, 24, 26 left, 86, 89 right, 97, 117, 121, 126, 130, 131, 132 bottom right, 137.